Martinis
&
Motherhood

TALES OF WONDER, WOE & WTF?!

Chrissy,
Raise your glass
to motherhood!
Cheers,
Lauren Stevens

Presented by

Shannon Day & Tara Wilson

Tipsy Squirrel Press
CANADA

Editors: Shannon Day and Tara Wilson
Copy Editor: Anne Radcliffe
Cover Designer: Daliborka Mijailović

Visit us online at www.tipsysquirrelpress.com.

Note from the Editors

Each essay is reflective of the conventions of its author's country of origin, as well as her personal voice, so you may notice variation in the spelling choices and styles throughout the book. It is our intention to preserve each contributor's individual style.

We feel it is important to mention that we are in no way condoning drinking during pregnancy nor are we encouraging alcohol abuse. This book is about embracing the good moments and celebrating triumph over the tricky ones. Please drink responsibly.

We're sure that you are going to find writers you love within these pages, both new discoveries and familiar favourites. Please visit the contributor pages on our website www.tipsysquirrelpress.com to find links to their blogs and to connect with them on social media.

If you enjoy our book, we'd be so appreciative if you could write a quick review on Amazon as it really helps with our promotion and marketing. Also, we'd love it if you'd share *Martinis & Motherhood* with your friends because great things happen when we share our tales of *Wonder*, *Woe* and *WTF?*! Thank you for your support.

We dedicate this book to all moms as they live their own tales of *Wonder, Woe and WTF?!*

May you have more *Wonder* than *Woe*, but just enough *WTF?!* to keep you laughing for years to come.

Table of Contents

Introduction

Martinis and motherhood go hand in hand, but not in a drown-your-sorrows sort of way. We view the relationship between mom and martini sort of like that of child and ice cream sundae. It's a treat! One that busy moms deserve to indulge in.

Martini (or mocktini) sipping is a celebratory and victorious act, best enjoyed in the company of fellow mom friends. Here, within the pages of *Martinis & Motherhood* you'll find heartstring-yanking stories of wonder, coffee-spewing tales of woe, and utterly ridiculous accounts of WTF?! all written by moms who are a lot like you. Each story is paired with a simple-to-make martini that looks fab and tastes divine, as well as a shareable toast to celebrate some of motherhood's many clink-worthy moments.

After the bums are wiped and the lunches are made; after the homework is done and the sheets have been changed; after we've chauffeured, escorted, worried to the max, had our sanity questioned, and our legs are still un-waxed; after we've kissed it all better, and bid them goodnight; we moms deserve to have something that's *just right*. Like a beautiful martini.

We hope that you enjoy our collection of martinis and toasts and that you'll see yourself and your own experiences in the tales that we share. We believe that great things happen when we open up to other moms about our own moments of *Wonder*, *Woe*, and *WTF?*! Happy reading!

Cheers!
Shannon & Tara

Tales of Wonder

These tales, insightfully written by some reflective moms (who aren't at all cheesy), are told with the wonderment and awe that only motherhood can bring. Each story is followed by a tasty martini recipe and an appreciative toast for you and your mom friends to share. Grab your tissues and don't bother shaving because tears and goosebumps are bound to occur.

Best Laid Un-Plans

Alison Huff

I was 25 years old, married for nearly three months, and my period was five days late. It had been an unpredictable beast of a thing for quite some time, a hormone-triggered anomaly that I had attributed to the planning of a roller coaster of a wedding. I had a lingering case of Post-Wedding Traumatic Stress Syndrome, I was sure of it. That's all it was, and nothing more.

My dear husband of 84 days wasn't so sure of that assessment. While looking into his eyes, I could see his doubt performing a jig with glee, like a silent rain dance that might water the seed he had successfully planted. He just knew that I was pregnant. I knew that I was not.

When he asked me to pee on a stick one early December morning, I humored him, because that's what wives are supposed to do. I was determined to prove him wrong, because that is also something that wives are supposed to do. Still naked, I begrudgingly rolled out of our bed and dutifully took the pregnancy test from his hand, sashaying my much-too-skinny ass into the bathroom and closing the door behind me.

Given the title of this book, I'm sure you can guess what my pee told me.

I stood at the bathroom sink, staring down in horrified disbelief at the plastic harbinger of my doom. A little pink "plus" sign stared back at me, and I swore it let out a menacing giggle.

Terror didn't quite describe the level of fear that coursed through my veins in that moment. I wasn't ready for motherhood. I was *nowhere* near ready. I had just gotten married. What did I know about being a parent? I couldn't even keep a rubber tree plant alive, so how in the hell could I ever be responsible for another human being?

I'm almost ashamed to admit this now, but knowing that there was a foreign body growing inside my own completely freaked me out. Like it or not, that thing was going to have to come out one day, THROUGH MY VAGINA. OH MY GODS! I recalled the birthing video I watched in eighth grade science class—the one that was so dangerous my parents had to sign a permission slip to allow me to view it. I knew what delivering a child looked like, and it defied the laws of nature. There was no way a baby was going to fit through there. It was simply impossible.

I was going to die.

I had been in the bathroom for a very long time, lost in morbid thought. As much as I wanted to keep time from moving forward, I knew I couldn't stay in the bathroom forever. "What goes in must come out" was apparently going to be the theme of the day.

When I finally opened the door, I saw my husband of 84 days patiently waiting on our bed, and I could not speak. I couldn't form the words to deliver my terrible news. While standing there in the doorway, still naked and at the most vulnerable I had ever been in my entire life, I broke down and cried. Wailed, really—like the world's most awkward banshee.

"It's okay," he said as he led me toward our bed and sat me down. He smiled and hugged me tightly. "It'll happen one day. It just wasn't time for a baby yet."

I was sobbing so hard that I began to hyperventilate. "I'M (wheeze!) ALREADY (wheeze! sniffle-snort-wheeze!) PREGNANT!"

My husband's smile turned into the giddy laughter of impending fatherhood. I really wanted to hit him because I did not think he understood what would be happening to me in a matter of months. What kind of sick bastard would find that amusing?

"Are you sure?" he asked. "We're having a baby? WE MADE A BABY!"

Yes, I was well aware of what we did.

"This is amazing! We're going to be parents! Breathe, Ali! Calm down and breathe; it'll be okay! Oh my God, I'm going to be a dad!" He continued to spew forth words of joy and happiness while doing his best to assure me that this was not the end of the world—it was the beginning of a new one. Eventually, my tears ran dry and my fears began to evaporate with them.

A tiny little speck of a creature was renting my one-womb apartment, and we had put it there. We made a life, he and I.

A life.

That was some profound stuff.

In that moment, I couldn't help but smile. I no longer worried about being pregnant or about the painful birthing process. I didn't panic about what kind of parent I would be or about the things I might totally screw up some day in the future.

I had stopped agonizing over all of those things because I was too thunderstruck to move beyond the notion that we *made* someone. Like wizards, we had conjured a brand new person into existence, a person who would have thoughts and feelings. And, one day, it would speak, and maybe it would grow up to be as sarcastic as I am, and it would love to dance as much as I do, and it would have my husband's musical ability, and… and…

I realized something: I could not wait to meet that person.

I couldn't wait to be a mom.

The Fearless

For moms who face and embrace the unplanned.

You'll need:

1 ½ oz. orange vodka (or use chilled orange flavoured sparkling water in place of vodka, for a mocktini)
1 oz. cranberry juice
1 oz. pineapple juice
½ oz. fresh lime juice
Cranberries and/or a slice of pineapple, for garnish

Method:

1. Fill a metal shaker with ice and add the above ingredients.
2. Shake until icy cold.
3. Strain into your martini glass.
4. Garnish with pineapple or drop a few cranberries into the glass, think brave thoughts, and enjoy.

Toast to morning pee, unplanned surprises, and motherhood without fear.

Purse Person, Plural

Jocelyn Pihlaja

The night before my son's twelfth birthday, he and I went on a spontaneous outing.

After driving to the shopping area in town, we groped bags of Legos and attempted to discern which mini-figures hid within the mystery packets. Our fingers worked to detect a unicorn horn. For my son to celebrate his birthday the next day while clutching a Lego unicorn would be, well, like being the forty-seven-year-old mother of a twelve-year-old clutching a Lego unicorn: THE APEX OF AWESOME.

Once we selected our bags of figures and were walking to the car, I noted that my purse's straps were frayed and on the verge of giving way entirely. Conveniently, we were near my favorite store.

"Hey, kiddo, I feel The Mothership calling. The computer chip in my brain that's linked to the main hive is pinging. Can we answer its call? Do you mind doing a little more dinkin' around before we head home?"

The immediate response confirmed his status as Best Playmate. "What are you asking? I *love* dinkin' around."

At The Mothership, we surveyed the square footage of purse. Hip to hip, we waded in.

"So, what kind of purse are you looking for, Mom?"

He posed a hard question. The criteria are variable so long as the purse speaks to me. It's a *love* thing.

"Well, you know the colors I like. Actually, even though I don't usually choose oranges and reds, I *could* do them in a purse. I would need to keep a red purse away from my red face, though, and the only time I can imagine my face nearing my purse would be when digging for a quarter, Kleenex, lip balm, Band-Aid, dental floss, car keys, phone, or wallet, so what I mean to say is no reds or oranges. Also, I really hate blingy stuff and decorative hardware feels *try hard*. Basically, we're looking for a classic purse without a lot of crap jammed onto it. Also, fringe is the devil's work."

Processing my words, the boy wandered over to a luscious navy blue dreamboat and gave it a heft. "How about this one? Nope, wait. It's open across the top, and you need a zipper so all your stuff doesn't spill."

Carry on, small man.

Moving to the next navy blue bag, he noted, "I like the shape of this one, and it's so soft. Do you need a long strap, or are short handles okay?"

Negotiable, kid. I won't know until I see it. It's a love *thing.*

Then he looked at the price tag. "Uh-oh. It's expensive. That's why it's so nice."

Teachable moment: You get what you pay for, buddy. Sometimes, when a purse is soft and shapely, that's because—much like your mother—it's well made.

"You should carry that one around for a little bit to test it out. Also, it's the last one, and you don't want anyone else to take it," he recommended.

I clutched it to my chest and petted the softness, just as I had petted this boy when he was a baby.

We wandered to the next display. "Yuck," he noted.

"Beiges and whites won't be practical. They'll get dirty so fast. Plus, they're boring, and you like fun. Keep walking."

Moving to the clearance rack, our eyes were drawn to a bright blue bag. It was smallish and zippered. "Ooh, I like that one," I squealed.

"But isn't it too small, Mom? Your wallet won't even fit."

"Ah, but I could use it when I travel and only need essentials—cash, credit card, lipstick, unicorn mini-figure. Those things would all fit!"

I grabbed the bright blue purse, smashed it against the navy blue one, and followed my young man.

Two feet later, I enthused, "Ooh, look! Isn't this one kind of nifty? The flap is asymmetrical, and it has two different chains for each shoulder strap!"

I'd gotten so off track, my counselor had to turn and give me a dead-on corrective stink eye. His gaze burned into mine as he countered the whimsy. "Mom. *No*. This purse is *red*. Would you say it's 'classic?' Can you undo that button on the flap easily? No, Mom. *No*."

He was right. In fact, rack after rack, every time I tried to derail my original intentions and get excited about the impractical or ridiculous, my adolescent's voice brought me back from the edge:

"When you put that one on, it juts out. You'll always be knocking things over with it. Since I'm always one step behind you, I could lose an eye."

"I don't think you should get two purses. That's expensive, and how many purses do you take out with you each day? ONE."

"You think that's cute now, but when you look at it next week, you'll realize it's ugly."

"That looks like a dead lizard on a string. You can't."

"I don't want to know someone who would carry that heap of sequins on her shoulder."

"Look at the lining inside that one. It will rip by Tuesday. And it looks like barf."

Then.

We turned a corner.

And saw.

The racks of green purses.

Green and I have a history. Green might actually be my son's father.

Our steps slowed; our fingertips grazed. Green was promising.

While I soaked in the big picture, the boy started digging to a barely visible hook in the back. "Mom! Look at this one! Lime green! And you know how we feel about lime green!"

I helped him extract it from the tangle of purses. It was lime green, all right.

"It doesn't have dangly junk or bling, either. Would it hold all your stuff? 'Cause, Mom? I think this is the one. This is the best one, right? Let's look at the price. Hey, not so bad! You *have* to get this one. LOOK AT THE GREEN! We love it; don't we love it?"

Fortunately, I'm open to lime green. Fortunately, it was a good size. Fortunately, it was a good price. Fortunately, it was well made. Fortunately, even if I'd been on the fence, unsure if the purse spoke to me or not, I realized that—on the cusp of my son's twelfth birthday—this was a moment to tuck into my heart. The next few years would see him moving further away from me, the two of us separating healthily and painfully. He would always be my boy, but he was about to become less and less *my* boy, and more and more the world's man. He would always be part of my pulse, yet I would miss him forever.

Rather than yielding to the wash of melancholy that threatened, I focused on what he was in that moment: in The Mothership, standing next to the green purses, enthusiastically holding up his choice.

Almost as tall as I, this young man was sweet, sensitive, funny, gentle, smart, observant, and intuitive. And he was applying all of his everything to helping me with my cause.

There was no question. Even if he'd been holding up a red purse dripping with sequins and fringe gilded with seven gold chains, I would have bought it.

It's a *love* thing.

The Perfect Purse

For moms with a stylist in the family.

You'll need:

2 oz. gin
¾ oz. freshly squeezed lime juice
Splash of soda water
A circular slice of lime, for garnish

Method:

1. Fill a metal shaker with ice and add the lime juice and gin.
2. Shake it up until it's nice and chilled.
3. Strain into your martini glass of choice.
4. Top it off with a splash of soda water, garnish with a circular slice of lime, contemplate purse shopping, and enjoy!

Toast to lime green purses, Motherships, and boys who shop with their moms.

A Mother's Wandering Mind of Wonder

Leigh-Mary Hoffmann

We weren't necessarily "trying," but we weren't "not trying" either. You get the point.

So, I wondered. That wonder was confirmed by eight at-home pregnancy tests. Yes, eight.

It was one of the most exciting days of my life.

I read. I planned. I picked out names. I picked out paint colors. I picked out a crib. I picked out bedding.

I felt. I connected. I knew.

I knew that this baby would bring a love like no other.

I also wondered.

I wondered what my baby girl would look like—would she have brown eyes like me or blue like her father? Would she be taller than her not-so-tall mom? What about her personality? I wondered about every single thing that I could wonder about this child.

And then my wonder spotlight shone on me.

I wondered what kind of mother I would be. I wondered if I was even ready for motherhood. I wondered if she would like me. I wondered and wondered and wondered. For 40 weeks, I wondered.

Then my world changed forever. Thirteen years ago, I became a mother for the first time. Thirteen years ago, anything that was wrong in the world—in my life—became right as I held my beautiful baby girl in my arms. She was perfect.

Mother's instinct whispered to me that she wasn't "typically perfect" according to milestone marker standards—you know, the ones listed on the questionnaire at the pediatrician's office. I felt like neon signs, which all seemed to be preaching "your child should be doing this and that by such and such an age," were blinding me everywhere I looked—in every parenting book I picked up and each magazine article I read. I had such a heavy heart ~~wondering~~ knowing—without officially *knowing*—that she wasn't "typically perfect." Except, she was better than that. She was imperfectly perfect.

Maggie toe-walked. She sat in the "W" position. She did not make much eye contact. She had low muscle tone and sensory issues. Her speech was delayed. If it was on the "be on the lookout for this" checklist, she ticked all the boxes. At the tender age of 18 months, my baby was diagnosed with PDD-NOS, an autism spectrum disorder.

At 18 months, Maggie would get on a mini-bus that picked her up in front of our home and brought her to a developmental preschool where she would receive Applied Behavior Analysis (ABA) therapy. Once home, there would only be a short period of rest before in-home special education, speech, and occupational therapists would occupy the rest of her day.

It didn't make sense. How did this happen? Her father is a smart man–he knows a lot about a lot. I did well in school and earned a college degree. We are both "normal." And doesn't autism affect boys more often than girls, anyway? That thought process of this first-time/uninformed parent was squashed, over time. In time, I began to understand. I began to understand not only autism, but more importantly, I began to understand my daughter and motherhood.

Maggie carried a plastic spoon in each hand. If not a plastic spoon—though that was her preference—she carried a small figurine. Sometimes, it was a figure so small you wouldn't even see it secured in her hands. When she wasn't grasping something tight, she wore stretchy winter gloves (the super small ones that expand to the size of your hand). Turns out, it wasn't entirely that she was quirky. She had sensory issues, and the feeling of gripping something tight was a sense of security. To this day, she will not wear certain fabrics, including denim jeans. We have about 20 pairs of leggings, and they're all that she will have touching her skin.

But it's not all about the quirks.

Maggie is a smart young woman, one who knows more about most things than most people know about some things. I know she will do great things in her life. As for her father and I being "normal?" Nope, not a chance. *None of us* are completely normal by society's standards; we ALL have our issues that make us different. Special. Quirky. Crazy. And as for autism being a gender game? While statistics show that, yes, more boys than girls are diagnosed, all are welcome to the team. Autism doesn't hold tryouts. If you qualify, you are automatically on the team–boy or girl.

I don't wonder why autism happened to my daughter. Instead, I wonder how I was chosen to be blessed with the gift of Maggie—my Maggie Sunshine. I wonder if other mothers know a love like this one. And then I wonder how I can even think such a question. A mother's love knows no boundaries. A mother's love simply… is.

It is a love of purity.

It is a love of rejoicing in the good times and comforting in the not-so-good times.

It is a love of holding. Of cuddling. Of crying. Of laughing. Of the day-to-day. Of the year-to-year. Of the minute-to-minute.

I do *still* wonder. I wonder… will my Maggie attend her high school prom? Will she ever have a best friend? Drive a car? Do typical things teens do that they're not supposed to do? I wonder, will she find the love of her life? Will she cherish a child as I do her?

I wonder… when I'm gone, who will take care of her? I wonder, will she be able to take care of herself? The wonder I felt before she came into this world is a wonder that has come full circle. My mothering mind of wonder is constantly wandering. But Maggie—my best friend and the first unconditional love I ever knew—will get me through. She always has.

Maggie is a wonder to behold: a gift from above for the world to learn from, admire and love. She is WONDERful.

The Wonderful

For moms of imperfectly perfect kids.

You'll need:

1 ½ oz. vodka
1 oz. triple sec
1 oz. grapefruit juice
½ oz. passion fruit juice
A slice of lime, grapefruit or an edible flower, for garnish

Method:

1. Fill a metal shaker with ice and add the above ingredients.
2. Shake this fab blend until it's really nice and cold.
3. Strain into your martini glass of choice.
4. Garnish with lime, grapefruit, or a quirky flower.

Toast to being quirky, to beating to the sound of your own drum, and to imperfectly perfect children.

Stealing Time

Louise Gleeson

We always put music on when we're in the kitchen. Today I'm standing at the stove, singing along, when I catch a flash of movement from my youngest child, who's having breakfast at the table.

She's still in her pajamas because our mornings together are slow. Everyone else has left for work and school. She's swinging her legs in time to the music, and I realize she has the only pair of feet in our family that can't reach the floor.

The back-and-forth motion of her dimpled feet brings up the memory of a blue clock and the ticking sound it made when the hands moved around its face. I found it when I was putting together our first nursery. It matched one of the accent colours in the rug on the nursery floor, and its sound reminded me of a clock in my grandmother's bedroom when I was a child. I thought it would be comforting.

I ended up hating that clock and resented how much time I spent watching it. The sound of it made my body tense; the sight of its hands moving in their never-ending circle played games with my sense of time.

Time never moved as quickly as I wanted it to.

I knew that wasn't the way I was supposed to feel. But first-time motherhood was hard. Convincing myself that I could make it to the next stage was hard. Enjoying my baby was hard.

When they put her into my arms for the first time, I felt like I had been thrown overboard. I spent those early months flailing as though I had forgotten how to swim. I used all my energy trying to swim against the current because I was convinced it would take me to the shore, where I would find solid ground to stand on.

But time did keep moving, and as the months passed, I paid less and less attention to counting it. Eventually, I learned to swim with the current instead of against. I started to use time to notice everything around me. I stopped worrying about when I would make it to the shore and started to focus more on finding the joy that comes with the journey.

I began to count the moments more than the minutes.

I remember when my daughter was six months old, and I was nursing her on the couch while I enjoyed a favourite show on TV. Sneaking downstairs instead of nursing in the rocking chair in her room had become our ritual on the days my husband had to work late. As I watched the light flicker across her closed eyes that night, I realized it was the first time I hadn't looked at the clock and felt resentment that we were alone.

I remember the first time my son sat on sand at the playground. I remember how closely I watched as he curled his toes around the sand and grabbed fistfuls to throw. His sister was climbing on the play structure nearby, and I realized that despite the challenges of getting two kids under the age of three to the park, I didn't want the afternoon to end.

I remember pulling into an outdoor garden centre to pick up summer plants for the backyard only days after our third baby was born. We had the windows rolled down. I watched the three of them in the rear-view mirror as a breeze came through and ruffled the kids' hair. I realized how much we had grown in what was beginning to feel like a very short time, and I wanted time to slow down.

I remember when we brought our youngest daughter home from the hospital; we were greeted with homemade "Welcome home!" banners and excited siblings dressed in "big brother" and "big sister" t-shirts. And I realized the heart could experience a collision of joy and sadness—I accepted that moment wouldn't ever happen again. I wanted time to stand still.

In this moment, I'm so glad those feet can't reach the floor. As I stand and watch them swing, I can hardly remember the version of myself that was convinced what was coming would be better than what was already there.

In those early days, time was something I wished away. Now I wish I could get it back.

I'm not needed in the same ways these days. I'm still caring for my children, of course, but I spend a lot more time as a spectator than as a participant in their day-to-day lives. I am finally standing on that shore, and they are swimming towards their own horizons without me.

I lift my hand whenever they look for me, however, with a smile of encouragement and a wave of support. In my other hand, I hold the memories of moments I've gathered like pebbles. Some are smooth and perfect; others are broken and jagged. Each one of them marks time more than the hands of a clock ever could.

I like that song, Mama. Can we listen to it one more time?

I walk across the room to press rewind and wish it could be that simple.

Of course we can, baby. We've got lots of time.

Moments Martini

For moms who turn minutes into moments.

You'll need:

1 ½ oz. vodka (omit for a mocktini)
1 cup diced watermelon
5 fresh mint leaves
Half a canned (or fresh, peeled) peach
A few ice cubes
Small triangular slice of watermelon or some mint, for garnish

Method:

1. In a blender, puree vodka, watermelon, peach, ice, and mint.
2. Pour into your martini glass of choice.
3. Garnish with a watermelon slice or some mint (or both), pull up a seat, and capture a few moments while you sip.

Toast to the beginning, middle, and end of each day. May the minutes always be moments.

The Donkey Is Strong in This One

Magnolia Ripkin

My teenage daughter is slim, coltish, and carries no shadows in her heart. She is so shiny. My young son is sensitive, sweet, and contrary like a brick wall. He thinks deeply and holds his heart far inside of himself. Both of them are a constant source of amazement to me just because they are mine. I cannot believe that my man and I made these two fully-functional humans. That is every parent's view, of course, but what makes them even more fascinating is seeing the evidence of our collection of genetic building blocks carried forward through time to form these two wonders of nature.

When I look at my kids, I see threads of their heritage running through them so clearly. I am ever in awe that I can recognize the endless array of facial expressions, mannerisms, and other echoes of their ancestors. I can see where they got their intelligence, their strength, and so many physical attributes… including my unfortunate, freakishly large feet.

It is hard to imagine that the combined genes that form these two headphone-wearing sofa-loungers come from so far back through the history of our families. It seems like their ancestors, many years gone, simply reappear momentarily in the form of these two children. Either some traits have been inherited and passed on, or their great-grandparents have found a way to project themselves through time and the veil of death to make their spirits known.

I know how my parents felt when they first saw me get through a difficult kitchen table talk by smoothing the place mat in front of me. I was really young, but I still remember it. Three generations of my family looked at each other, agog, because they recognized that mannerism from my great-grandmother. When she had to hear or say hard things, place mats were straightened. This nervous habit emerged from the depths of my DNA chain. Now that I am a mother, I can appreciate how eerie that experience must have been for them.

There is so much we can learn about ourselves from the stories of our families. My people emigrated to escape the ravages of life on the losing side after World War II. There were soldiers, wise women, and wealthy business owners among my people. Turns out, the most powerful trait that made its way down through that bloodline is mouthy women. They were strong, brash, and usually well-endowed, and they were a constant worry to their fathers. I can see this trait in my daughter, and I also see how the gentleness of her papa's temperament acts as a counterbalance to the dragon's fire she carries from my side.

Both my grandmothers were shrewd and wily in the face of adversity. Fiercely protective mothers, they faced unspeakable trauma and danger. Both lived in besieged cities during World War II, yet they carried their families—relatively unscathed—through constant dangers from bombs, starvation, rape, and the loss of everything they had. There are stories of their bravery throughout our family.

My feisty Slavic grandmother faced down Russian soldiers to protect her daughters. Her dacha was about to be overrun and ransacked by invading armies. When they burst through her door, she demanded to speak with their Commandant. She was the type of woman who brooked no arguments from young soldiers, so the leader was brought to parley with her. She offered to slaughter and cook a giant sow and serve them all the wine in her cellar if they would leave her children unmolested. The deal was struck, and the soldiers left to carry on raping and pillaging their way through other villages, but our family survived and fled.

My other grandmother traded in the black market for coal and potatoes to keep her family warm and fed. When the allied forces bombed their house, they had just abandoned it. The other branch of my genetic thread remained intact.

The girl I am raising today has shown herself to be a determined champion of the underdog. She wields her great-grandmothers' moxie when she confronts high school mean girls. Her steely determination says, "I can bleed and hang a fully grown sow, and I can make it for dinner, too; you want to mess with me?"

My son is an exact replica of my husband. We have traced my husband's side back to the early Loyalists leaving the newly-born USA to settle in Upper Canada. So many generations back, my husband's people were staunch in their beliefs and were willing to fight for their motherland, regardless of history's judgement of them. I see that residual determination in my children; its genetic footprint has stubbornly lasted since the 1700's. It is why we often say, "The donkey is strong in this one."

I used to wonder about my son's skin. Technically, he is Caucasian, but only until mid-June of each year. Then he becomes a creature of exotic dark pigment seemingly after just moments in the sun. We have recently discovered, a few generations back, a lineage that has an Aboriginal ancestor who married a settler. She has left a trace of her beauty and sensitivity to her environment in my son, his father, and his grandfather.

The timbre of our voices is another interesting and unique hallmark we all carry as speaking great apes. The precise tone of a long-gone grandparent coming from the mouth of my children gives me a lump in my throat. I miss my elders a little less when I have just heard something they would have said. Maybe if I was a believer in that which I can't see or prove, I would feel like I have been visited by the shadow of my grandfather when my son talks like him.

My grandfather brings to mind the smell of sawdust and coffee as he worked at his trade. Our side of the family has a carpentry gene, and although it has skipped me entirely, I see it in my daughter, who loves to create and build. She does so with such care and attention that there must be a hand resting on her shoulder as she sands the rough edges of wood. Her generation also builds software and makes movies with creative scripts and wicked-smart editing. I wonder which pool of genetic features and options that one came from. Maybe it was the early cave-painters who set the stage for modern movies.

When I look back at all that made me, and subsequently my children, I feel the fire of single-minded ferocity that I carry in myself. I also watch for it in my children. They will need to be strong and resilient as they navigate their lives. They are both going to have to be warriors for all the right causes: equity, peace, tolerance, their natural world, and for love and family. What their genes haven't given them, we will have to teach them. I am hoping the mix of genetic materials is a healthy one, and that it brings the best of many generations into theirs.

I could spend a long time getting lost in my thoughts about the fullness of time and our place as the passers-on of genes. I am snapped back to the present when I watch my husband and son deeply focused on something, both with their tongues sticking slightly out of the side of their mouths, completely unaware of how their thread ties together.

The Granny

For moms who appreciate their family roots.

You'll need:

2 oz. vanilla vodka
1 oz. sour apple schnapps
½ oz. melon liqueur
Slice of green apple for garnish

Method:

1. Fill a metal shaker with ice and add the above ingredients.
2. Shake until the mixture is perfectly chilled.
3. Strain into a fabulous martini glass, garnish with apple, think of the wonderful donkeys in your own family, and enjoy.

Toast to elders, babies, and the threads that connect us.

A Mother's Intuition

Angila Peters

The due date. Mine was November 21st. How robotic it would sound, in retrospect, as the standard response to all questioning do-gooders for ten whole months.

November 30th arrived, and I was still pregnant. That made me more than overdue; it meant returning all the birthstone trinkets I'd purchased, and let me tell you, I don't keep receipts.

I waited six long years for my husband to be ready for children and marriage; I was not waiting a second longer.

Like all rational pregnant women, I devised an "out." Birth plan be damned, I insisted on induction. Nipple squeezing, castor oil shooters, and squats were for patient people.

Pitocin kicked my ass, my uterus, and my baby out of there.

She arrived at 5:30 p.m., on the last possible day of November, to an obvious control freak of a mother who would do no such thing as have a baby in December.

As my eyes greeted hers, I didn't want to be

anywhere else on Earth.

The first child is your everything. That means you can sit, without others to distract you, and soak up every little move they make. And that's all I did after leaving the hospital.

I was a mother. The overwhelming responsibility and love shifted me into a dimension I'd never known. I feared and embraced this newfound wonder and allowed time to disappear.

It had been three weeks since I'd left the house. I was content to write grocery lists and hand them off. I could stay cozy in the comfort of my zone forever with this baby, but it was finally time to remove my maternity sweats and trade them for my maternity jeans.

On December 21st, we headed out on our first shopping excursion.

Christmas was coming, and last-minute gifts were a great excuse to rejoin the world. We piled into the car. My husband drove, and my mom attended to coos and whimpers in the back seat. I sat under the world's largest diaper bag filled with—in hindsight—way too much stuff.

It felt good to see the light again, but an overwhelming dread hit me as soon as we pulled out of the driveway. I started crying. Hysterically. Both my mom and husband looked at me like I was half funny, half crazy. Even I was a little embarrassed at my outburst.

I just didn't feel safe.

But I swallowed it down, and we pressed on. I had to trust that being in a car was normal. Mood swings and high emotions are normal post-pregnancy occurrences. But intuition of danger was not something I was knowingly gifted at until this day.

After picking up a few items and letting my mom spoil her first grandchild, we were starving. Shopping *and* eating out. What a big day!

After turning left at a four-way stop, a police motorcycle zoomed on by. Not out of the ordinary. We lived in a busy city. It sped ahead and left my mind.

In the next fragment of time, I looked up to see a white utility van flying into my side of the car. My daughter was right behind me.

I saw it coming. I only had time to scream my husband's name. He never saw it.

As for most people who describe moments like this, time stands still. You see glass slowly shattering like a beautiful art form. You hear the thumping of your heart, beating in fear, as if you were alone in the pit of a drum. You see life fly out of your grasp.

And when the pause button is released, reality forces a slap to your face that snaps you out of a trance.

Or maybe that was the airbag.

Instinctively, I wiggled my toes. They worked. Microseconds later, I realized we had been in a crash. The baby was all I could think of, and I realized that I was pinned and couldn't turn around. I wanted to hide and disappear. I didn't want to see anything horrible. I didn't want to lose something I had only seconds ago.

I looked left, and I saw my husband was alive. And then there was a man at our window with a gun, yelling at us to get down.

Make this not real. Please stop.

What I didn't know, in that moment, was that the man with a gun was an undercover officer, and my husband had already been screaming to check our child. I also didn't know that my angel mother had thrown herself over our daughter.

And then I heard my baby cry. People were assuring me that she was all right. Breathing returned to my body.

We'd been hit by a stolen vehicle. None of that made sense at the time. What I knew was my baby was okay, and that only a half-second difference could have killed us both.

The ambulance attendants did not have my cooperation until I saw my daughter. They placed her next to me and drove to the hospital. She was crying, and my milk came in. Feeling that brought me back to my body and to the pain of the impact. Any time before becoming a mom, I would have complained. I would have demanded drugs. Anything. But all I wanted to do was feed her and see for myself that she was all right.

Once we were in the hospital, I needed to be examined and have glass removed from my arm. Having never before experienced such trauma, or an innate need to have my child in my arms, I refused to do much until I could breastfeed. I needed to smell and feel her. I needed my couch and the safety of home.

What I learned, far too soon, was that the child I feel such deep, primal love for could be taken away in a blink and that a mother's intuition is very real.

That day also made me break my "don't drink while breastfeeding" rule.

The accident gave me permission to listen carefully to the inner tugging. The small whispers that moms get. The ones that raise a flag of awareness. Sometimes it makes me overcautious, and it's hard to know when I'm being more afraid than aware.

I'd like to say that it also blessed me with the patience and understanding to be a better mom. But after the dust settles and the trauma subsides, your kids make you crazy, they misbehave, and you yell at them sometimes.

Those moments are the true gifts, because your child is there with you.

Life goes on.

Primal Love

For moms who just know.

You'll need:

1 ½ oz. vodka
1 oz. lychee liqueur
2 oz. white cranberry juice
A lychee, a slice of lime, or a few cranberries, for garnish

Method:

1. Fill a metal shaker with ice and add the above ingredients.
2. Shake, shake, shake and strain into a fabulous martini glass—you'll know which is the right one!
3. Garnish with a lychee, a slice of lime or drop a few cranberries into the glass.
4. Now, light a gorgeous candle, put your feet up, and enjoy.

Toast to protecting our babies, to mother's intuition, and to knowing when to listen to our inner voice.

Life Is Like a Bowl of Ramen Noodles

Lauren Stevens

On a cold and rainy fall day, cabin fever growing like the puddles outdoors, I had the opportunity to introduce my son to one of my favorite college food staples: ramen noodles (snatched from my husband's secret pantry stash). I watched Declan marvel at the length of the noodles. He giggled as he dangled the ribbons over his mouth, caught each fried and freeze-dried starchy length between his lips, and slurped it up in one go. I couldn't help but join in his excitement.

It wasn't long before I was sharing noodles with my son and trying to catch individual noodles in my mouth. Each of us pulled random noodles from the bowl, trying to see who could get the longest and squiggliest on each attempt. Oh, how we laughed!

In that moment, it struck me how many ordinary things became extraordinary when viewed through my son's eyes.

Before that fall day, ramen noodles had simply been a cheap food I consumed after a night of drinking in college. I would drunkenly devour uncooked noodles as I waited impatiently for my hot pot to heat the water to rehydrate them. Those noodles, long since removed from my diet, were what I ate in my college dorm room on days when I was battling a cold or feeling blue in the thick of the frigid winters of northwestern Pennsylvania's Snow Belt.

Dreary Erie was a nickname borne from truth as the sun disappeared in late October and magically reappeared sometime in April. Winter dumped snow in accumulations measured in feet rather than inches. Unwilling or unable to slog through whiteouts, blizzards, and slush to the cafeteria, I would boil a batch of ramen noodles. With the help of those grease-and-sodium-laden noodles, I would add another pound towards the ever-feared freshman fifteen.

Almost twenty years later, on a damp and blustery fall day, those same noodles were a lesson in food play and fun with my son.

At two years old, Declan's personality becomes more pronounced with each day. Every trip outside of the house is a cause for wonderment and awe, no matter how mundane the errand. Grocery runs are an adventure; Declan begs to visit the fish counter or to explore fruits and vegetables in the produce section. Before, grocery shopping had always been a perfunctory errand. I would zip through the aisles, list in hand, with the objective of getting in and out as fast as possible (so I could check another errand off my list). These days, grocery shopping is an eye-catching and educational outing full of explanations and the possibility of new taste experiences.

Taking a day trip to the beach—with its myriad sights, sounds, and smells—brings back childhood memories for both my husband and myself and creates memorable moments in our family's timeline. The act of picking blueberries in an orchard—of being covered in the vibrant purple juice and popping every other berry into his mouth—is a sensory experience that I know will trigger fond memories for my son when he grows older. Even eating a meal in a restaurant becomes something new and fascinating. As Declan sits, ordering for himself, he's able to assert his newfound independence, experimenting with language in the presence of strangers.

It's a joy to watch my son's exuberance when we go into the city and how he comes alive amidst the constant motion, sounds, and people bustling around him. Trips to our local zoo inspire curious questions for days afterwards. Even a simple walk in our backyard and the neighboring fields becomes exotic when contemplating the possibilities of wild raspberry bushes; the carpet of black walnuts beneath the lush, green canopy; and the many shapes of twigs and branches that fall from the abundance of trees.

And mud puddles? Look out, because there are hours of enjoyment and exploration to be had there! Perhaps my favorite activity with Declan is going to bookstores. I can share in his excitement of the thousands of possibilities on the shelves and how each spine hints at a new adventure.

So many parents talk about how having children changes them—how they learn about a love they never knew existed. They talk about how parenting teaches true selflessness and how to channel a patience they never before possessed. I reflect on my pre-parenthood years and am struck by how blind I was to the world around me. If there is one thing my son has taught me, it is to slow down, take in my surroundings and give myself over to each experience—no matter how mundane or insignificant it may seem.

Viewing the world through my child's eyes has been—and continues to be—one of the greatest pleasures of motherhood. Declan's innocence reminds me to be grateful for life's blessings, no matter the size. It allows me to practice my inherent inquisitiveness and to sate my own curiosity about the world around me.

Despite the horrors on the nutrition label, I will always look upon ramen noodles fondly, remembering how a shared bowl on a cold and rainy day inspired me to reflect on how beautiful my life is as a mother.

The "Life is Like..."

For moms who stop and smell the noodles.

You'll need:

3 oz. gin
1 oz. sake
6 slices of cucumber

Method:

1. Fill a metal shaker with ice; add the ingredients and 5 slices of cucumber.
2. Shake it up and strain into a chilled martini glass.
3. Garnish with a slice of cucumber, breathe in the deliciousness, and enjoy.
4. Oh, and plug in the kettle for tonight's ramen noodle dinner.

Toast to noodles, nostalgia, and nascent dreams.

Of Woman Grown

Shannon Drury

Pregnancy is deeply weird. It plays tricks on both body and mind. As your breasts swell, as your belly thickens, and as your hips widen, your sense of reality warps. One day, eyeball-deep in estrogen (and the copy of *What to Expect When You're Expecting* you grabbed at Savers), you truly believe that yours is the only pregnancy that matters, has ever mattered, or *will* ever matter—in all the history of creation.

My copy of *What to Expect*, the 1988 edition, featured a portrait of a placid white woman in a flowered muumuu gazing dreamily into space from a wooden rocking chair. In new editions, the slim and fashionable mom-to-be on the cover looks like she's just freshened up after a vigorous session of Pilates, and there is still no asterisk on the book leading you to fine print that says "*Baby body and mental health results may vary."

Maybe there should be. That brief, cautionary note might have prepared me—a stubbornly rational atheist six months pregnant with my first child—for the near-religious experience I had as I was clutching a bottle of

Metamucil in the aisles of a Minneapolis Cub Foods.

The "enlightenment" began with a visit to my obstetrician, a woman of science who explained some of my bodily changes in Darwinian terms. "The theory is," Dr. Farber said, "that your morning sickness is steering you away from eating something that's bad for the baby."

"But I had to throw up after I brushed my teeth," I said. "Toothpaste isn't bad for the baby… is it?"

Dr. Farber shook her head with that *first-timers are so paranoid!* look on her face—a look that was becoming increasingly familiar to me. "The smell of the toothpaste was so strong you couldn't stand it, I bet," she said. I nodded. "That's your cavewoman DNA at work. It can't tell the difference between toothpaste and rotting meat. You might want to try brushing with baking soda for a while."

Then Dr. Farber took a look at the clipboard that her nurse left behind. "That's interesting," she said, clicking back her retractable pen. "You put on a bit of weight this month."

"Wasn't I supposed to?"

She scratched a few notes into my file. "Eleven pounds in four weeks is, well…" I watched as she struggled to form a reply that wouldn't result in a potentially baby-threatening surge in my blood pressure. "Let's just say that it's somewhat *more* than necessary."

I thought for a moment. Did I misinterpret her advice to eat bulk-forming popcorn with my prenatal vitamin? I had so little left to enjoy these days. No alcohol. No caffeine. No regular bowel movements. Dr. Farber handed me a pamphlet titled *Pregnancy Nutrition and You,* a title that already implied that the two were in opposition to one another. Even worse, the beaming mother in the pamphlet photograph didn't look puffy and bloated like I did. With her slightly distended belly, she looked like she'd just had her fill of unlimited breadsticks at The Olive Garden.

A dangerous thought entered my dizzy, hormonal brain: maybe the pregnant do *not* have free rein to consume massive amounts of foods that sensible people restrict—like Laffy Taffy, glazed donuts and Orville Redenbacher's Movie Theater Popcorn Now with Extra Butter.

With a gentle tone, in response to my obvious first-timer's panic, Dr. Farber suggested that I make an effort to limit the junk food, including the bulk-forming popcorn. "Instead, get yourself a bottle of Metamucil at the grocery store. You can drink a teaspoon or two of that when you're backed up. THAT should blow your pipes out in no time!" she added with the cheerful aplomb of a woman intimately familiar with various forms of human discharge.

I waddled off into the cold, cruel world once more, determined to spend my trip at the grocery store in the laxative and vegetable aisles only. I would take pains to avoid anything in cartoonish packaging.

Like every late afternoon, the store overflowed with harried commuters picking up dinner. Some were dragging fussy children just picked up from daycare or school. I couldn't help but watch them as the kids smeared their marker-streaked hands all over the stacks of Diet Sprite. Mothers barked at them to quit it, and I sighed happily, daydreaming.

These kids, just a short time ago, were in their mamas' bellies. I looked towards a squalling three-year-old being chastised for stealing walnuts from the bulk bin. *She was in that mama's belly once.*

And on it went. *So was he. So was she.*

A few kids later, it hit me. *Every single person in this store was grown in a woman's belly.*

The stooped janitor with the thick glasses who was sopping up broken jars of juice and spaghetti sauce: *he grew in a woman.*

The young checker at register four, her head and neck covered by a silken hijab that matched the dark green of her Cub-issue jacket: *she grew in a woman.*

The thick-necked security guard with a haircut so high and tight that his ears resembled a pair of curling, pink bicycle handlebars: *he grew in a woman too.*

Not every woman will grow a baby, but every single person in existence, every person that ever was or will be, was grown by a woman.

I felt faint. A thin layer of sweat appeared on my forehead. If I were religious, I might have a plausible claim that the Virgin Mary herself, Mother of all Mothers, cradled my face in her slender, bloodless hands. That she floated down to the produce department of Minneapolis Cub Foods *just* for the sole purpose of giving me this epiphany. Every estrogen-soaked cell in my body exploded outward in a quantum-level Big Bang and then contracted back into my 174 pound mortal shell with the collective insight of one hundred universes.

Like I said, pregnancy is deeply weird.

But as I paid the hijab-clad former fetus for my powdered fiber and bag of Haralson apples, the moisture on my face and beneath my armpits dried, my terror lessened, and I felt a weight lift. The weight didn't lift from my belly or from my hips (that wouldn't "lift" for three more months), but it did lift from my anxious, first-timer's heart.

If all these people grew in women's bellies, then my pregnancy—though still a big deal—might not be so precious that any little thing could derail it.

"Could you hold on a second?" I asked the checker as she announced my total. I reached behind me, past the copies of tabloid magazines with scrawny TV stars on their covers, and I grabbed a package of KitKat bars. "I'd like to get this too, please," I said as I dropped the candy on the black vinyl conveyor belt. "I'm growing a person in here." My checker nodded, with amusement and more than a little sympathy. Her face told me that she, too, was a mother.

The Deeply Weird

For moms who marvel at the circle of life.

You'll need:

1 oz. popcorn vodka
1 oz. butter ripple schnapps
1 oz. white chocolate liqueur
½ oz. cola
Shredded chocolate, crushed popcorn pieces and/or crumbled cookies, for the rim

Method:

1. On your plate, put your rim toppings: shredded chocolate, crushed popcorn pieces and/or cookie crumbs. Using syrup, or butter ripple schnapps, wet the rim of the glass and then spin the rim into the toppings.
2. Fill a metal shaker with ice and add the vodka, schnapps, liqueur and cola.
3. Shake until the mixture is chilled and frothy.
4. Strain into your rimmed martini glass, contemplate the circle of life, and enjoy.

Toast to the women who grew us—may they be sane, safe, and *regular*.

The Saga of the Socks

Sarah Deveau

I promise you, this is an essay on wonder, though it took some woe to get there.

I can't pinpoint exactly when we began to notice how different our middle daughter, Jackie, was from her two easygoing sisters. Instead of eagerly anticipating a new adventure, whether it was meeting new people or checking out an unfamiliar playground, Jackie would pepper us with questions. "Where are we going? Will I know anyone? Why can't we go somewhere I know I'll like?"

Dropping her off at daycare required a complicated goodbye routine that involved handshakes, fist bumps, kisses, and hugs in a specific order. She cried frequently and was excessively clingy, even in the comfort of our own home.

She was the kid who had to be pried from my arms on the first day of kindergarten—and every day afterward for the entire month of September.

In October, a note came home from the school. With winter approaching, Jackie (who had lived in Crocs without socks for the whole of her five-year existence) would have to wear socks to school and in class.

Easier said than done.

I bought basic socks from a big box store. "They bug me!" she wailed, desperately yanking them off the moment my back was turned. I flipped them inside out, but her shoes still pressed the seams against her feet. No go. I let her choose character socks, socks with sparkles, socks with lace, and socks meant for little boys. Nope. "They bug me!"

She didn't have to wear socks, did she? If her feet weren't cold enough for her to complain, why did she need to wear socks? Then a second note came home. "Jackie must wear socks in school. Her foot odour has been commented on by the other students."

Ouch. No mom wants her kid to be the stinky one, so back to the store we went. Over $50 worth of socks went into the cart, and an hour later, they all went into her younger sister's sock drawer. They all failed the test.

We made a fourth trip to the store, and I became the mom that retail employees hate: the one that surreptitiously opens packages to try on socks in an attempt to avoid purchasing inevitable rejects.

We went home empty handed, but there, a package had arrived. Someone had anonymously (my money's on Grandma) sent us seamless socks from an online store. At $10 a pair, I hoped they would work. I wondered if I could sew GPS tracking devices into these exorbitantly priced socks.

Jackie tried them on and beamed up at me. "They work! I can wear these!"

My elation was short-lived. Before I had even had the chance to order more, they had been through the wash and were now "too rough."

I promise, I'm getting to the wonder soon.

We headed back to the big box store and ended up in

the women's sock aisle. At my wit's end, I was contemplating buying her granny-style knee-hose with no toe seams. That's when she spotted no-show socks (the kind meant to be worn with ballet flats). They were available in bright colours, appeared to have no seams, and at just $3 a pair, they wouldn't require me to take out a second mortgage. She tried them on. Success!

Jackie had socks she would wear... though only long enough to get to and from school. After that, they would be removed and shoved into jacket pockets or the bottom of her backpack.

I can laugh at the saga of the socks, now, because I have enough distance from the ordeal. In all honesty, though, I am ashamed at how frustrated I would get with my sweet little girl for not just wearing regular damn socks like her sisters and every other kid. "Whiny," "wimpy," and "wuss" were the words that would pinball around my mind as we shuffled through socks aisles in store after store.

Days and months passed. And, as Jackie learns to express herself with words more than wails, I've discovered there's an incredibly wondrous side to her sensitive personality.

Once, when we dropped my dad off at the airport after a visit, she sobbed quietly in the back seat the whole way home. For days after, I would stumble upon her snuffling in her room because she missed her granddad so much. After his most recent visit, she insisted we wake her at 5 a.m. so she could see him off at the airport.

Now I know that it wasn't just about the socks. I was frustrated and worried about her fearfulness and her anxiety. As a grab-life-by-the-horns extrovert and unflappable optimist, I couldn't relate to this timid child who was always so quick to cry.

This kid, our wacky Jackie, feels *all* the feels, no matter whether they are the seams on her socks or the love she has for her family and friends. She has a boundless ability to give love and kindness to everyone in her circle. Friends and teachers comment on what a generous spirit she has, how affectionate she is, and how astounding her compassion for others is.

Jackie has taught me—and still teaches me every day—how to slow down. She taught me how to listen with kindness, and she taught me to appreciate her open heart. If the price of having such a tender-hearted child in my life is a paycheque's worth of tissues for tears and socks without seams, I'm happy to pay up.

The Shrinking Violet

For moms raising sensitive souls.

You'll need:

1 oz. violet syrup
2 oz. vanilla vodka
A few mint leaves
Some violet petals or fresh mint, for garnish

Method:

1. Fill a metal shaker with ice; add violet syrup, vanilla vodka, and mint leaves.
2. Shake, shake, shake it up (in the closet of course so it doesn't hurt sensitive ears) and strain into a lovely martini glass.
3. Garnish with some violet petals and/or mint, put your sockless feet up, and enjoy.

Toast to socks without seams, pants without tags, and love with soft edges.

We Could Stay Here All Day

Tricia Mirchandani

Hinges turning, metal sliding against metal, the air shifting along the hallway with a soft *whoosh*—these are the sounds that stretch my lips into their first smile of the day. These are the sounds of my daughter opening her bedroom door.

Yes, as I hear the familiar creak that means she is ready to greet the day, I soften into a smile of joy. There is joy in seeing her in the hazy light of morning, peace that comes with even the briefest moment in this soft, waking space.

I breathe a sigh of relief when she rises on her own. Oh, I could never deny the blood we share. It is right there: in her nose, her cheeks, and the shape of her eyes. You see me in her every thread, but never more so than the way she must be pulled into daylight. She resists waking up, white-knuckling her bed and faking slumber to steal a few more minutes, even seconds, in the world of her dreams—that is all me. Most days, I reluctantly open my eyes to the world twice: once on my own, and once a few hours later with a smaller, darker version of myself.

She is me.

So I smile when I hear the door creak open because it means that today, on this morning, I won't have to fight her dreams and beg them to release her. I won't have to sit on her bed, gently shaking her into the world, when really I'd rather just curl up next to her.

When I glance up, I see a head of dark, bed-tousled hair peeking around the doorway. "Good morning, Mommy."

"Good morning, my love," I reply.

She pauses and then ambles across the room to where I sit. I reach out my arms, and she climbs into my lap, wrapping her long, bony limbs around me. I rest my cheek against her hair and breathe in that particular, fleeting scent of childhood in the morning.

"How did you sleep?" I ask.

"Good," she mumbles into my hair.

"Have any dreams?" I ask.

She shifts in my lap, trying to see my face while still attempting to curl into my nook. At five, she barely fits anymore, but neither of us is ready to admit that. So somehow we manage. She rests her head on my shoulder, her legs curled underneath her.

"Yes," she says, a faint smile teasing her cheeks.

I'm acutely aware, in moments like this, of the way the day pulls at me. The day will, if I let it, drag me away from the quiet and the cuddling. There are breakfasts to eat and bags to pack; there's school to get to and errands to run. Although I will say I'd happily sit there all day with her curled up next to me and our limbs tangled, the truth is that usually I feel antsy. I feel antsy to leave the minute I run out of things to say. The drill sergeant in my head runs a tight ship and she gets up in my face when I dilly-dally. Sometimes I don't even try to ignore her when she barks orders.

But on this particular morning, the one that started with smiles and ease, I tune the drill sergeant out. For much longer than I usually have the will to, I resist the urge to jump up and move us into the day. Instead, I hug my little girl—my little self. As I squeeze her, I feel how much we need this moment. She needs my hugs and cuddles. She needs to sit in my lap, no matter how uncomfortably, without fear of being tossed. She needs this time for her development, her self-esteem, and for connecting to one of her life's truest sources of love.

Sometimes, I forget how I need it too. I need it to renew the spirit of motherhood and to release the tensions of life. I need it to remind me that, although the world is enormous and growing all around me, the truth of my life is here in these incredibly short moments. They're in the long, bony limbs that are longer than I remember every time we come together. They're in the dark hair that smells of her and whiffs of lavender. This is where I find my center.

As if hearing my thoughts, she raises her little-girl voice to respond.

"I just want to stay here all day!"

"All day?" I smile.

"Yes!" she says with all the certainty of a five-year-old (which, of course, is more certainty than you'll find among any five hundred adults).

"What if you get hungry?"

"Then we'll go downstairs, get some food, and bring it right back here!"

"What if you have to pee?"

"The bathroom is right there!" she points.

"Won't you get bored?"

"There's toys up here!" she waves her hands around as if conjuring playthings out of the air.

And I smile. I smile because on this morning she woke on her own, and I didn't have to pull her out of her dreams. I smile because she came and curled up in my lap, and we sat there for a breath longer than our schedules allow. I smile because this won't happen again today—this time for the two of us to sit together. We won't get a chance to recapture the world that is now a lifetime away, when it used to be just the two of us all the time. I smile because I used to think we'd never find ways to reconnect again after her brother was born, when my attention became divided, and everything had to be shared—even my lap and time on it.

I smile because she's got it all figured out. We really could stay here all day.

Sweet Mornings

For moms who cherish morning snuggles.

You'll need:

2 oz. vodka
2 oz. freshly squeezed grapefruit juice
A splash of simple syrup (equal parts water and sugar brought to a boil, stirred until sugar dissolves and then cooled)
A slice of grapefruit, for garnish

Method:

1. Fill a metal shaker with ice and add all of the above ingredients (alternatively, mix ingredients, with only a few ice cubes, in a blender).
2. Shake (or blend) and serve in a martini glass.
3. Garnish with a grapefruit slice, steal one last snuggle, and enjoy.

Toast to mornings, to dilly-dally, and to capturing moments with your mini-me.

Note Yes, this martini is called Sweet Mornings but we don't recommend starting your day with one.

Abuelo in Our Hearts

Cordelia Newlin de Rojas

We were moving again. I could no longer remember the number of times I'd taped boxes together and struggled with what I should and shouldn't pack. It gets easier in some ways; don't bother moving microwaves and hold on to a good blender for dear life. But this move was different. My kids were now old enough to understand what was happening.

They knew they were leaving their friends. They had to say goodbye to their dog who couldn't come with us. I'd forced them to sort through their toys and pick at least five to give away to our local orphanage. I subsequently snuck out another two cartons of toys after tossing chocolates into a room, turning on the TV, and closing the door. International containers are expensive even for short hops.

It wasn't an easy decision to make, disrupting their lives like this, even if I knew it was the right one. I hoped that I was teaching them to let go of the things that don't matter too much (like the 461 bits of paper cut out from shopping mall catalogues) while teaching them what does count. A new job in a new country would allow Papa to spend much more time with them and we'd have a whole new place to explore.

Despite the obvious positives, these moves come at a high price.

In preparation for our move, I was sorting through our CDs—also known as dust magnets—when my youngest daughter, Claude, reached out for one of the few we've actually listened to—a Christmas special by Andrea Bocelli. She ran her fingers over the cover and begged me to play it. I tried dismissing her, desperate to check this task off my moving "to-do" list. But she was relentless.

She started sobbing that she wanted to hear the Abuelo song, but I had no idea what song she was talking about.

Abuelo was my father-in-law. Claude had never met him. He died when she was just sixteen months old and we were living on the other side of the planet. She knows of him, mostly thanks to a framed photograph we have of him holding her older sister, Pacifique, who was only ten months old at the time of the photo.

My brain was rapidly running over every permutation of what she could be referring to. We didn't have an Abuelo song, as far as I knew. But hell hath no fury like a misunderstood toddler. I began shouting out songs that we sang with my mother-in-law over Skype.

"No! No! No!" she kept insisting, "The music where *Abuelo* sings!" I still couldn't figure it out. She'd never met him. He'd never sang to her.

She was soon weeping and heaving. "Please! Play it!" And I was so stressed, trying to find the answer, that I missed her little hand pushing the CD into mine.

Finally, at the speed of Sherlock in a tub of molasses, I put the pieces together. I looked down at Andrea Bocelli and then over to our Day of the Dead altar, still up four months later, and I saw the resemblance. Andrea, all dressed in white, looked like an angel. He looked like our Abuelo.

Times like that really test the choices I've made as a mother. In that moment, I thought about spring, 2011, when we had decided to travel to France (to see my family) instead of Mexico (to see my husband's). It was going to be our first holiday home since our big move across the globe. Our eldest, Pacifique, was just three at the time, and our baby was to be one at the end of the summer. France was a 13-hour direct flight. Mexico was, at minimum, three flights and 48-72 hours of travel with stopovers. Tickets to Mexico were pricier. We only had two weeks.

We chose France. I figured my in-laws would take the opportunity to visit us there.

As our departure date approached, I overheard a concerned call between my husband and his parents. Afterward, he hung up the phone and told me they wouldn't be coming to France. His father was going to start radiation and possibly chemotherapy. Again. Abuelo had already vanquished a few bouts of cancer. One day we would see it was a case of whack-a-mole: as soon as one was beaten back, another one would crop up. But we didn't know this at that time. Abuelo was otherwise on the young side, always positive and full of wise advice. I had been sure he would outlive us all.

We agreed we would come to Mexico that following summer as such a long a trip would be too much right now. But there was one moment when a ray of clarity struck me. I told my husband we should go to Mexico instead. But he knew how much I wanted to see my mother and how tired I was since the big move and the birth of our second. He knew I was struggling and *so* looking forward to handing over the baby to relatives whilst stuffing my face with cheese, pâté, and copious amounts of wine.

He assured me it would be fine to go to Mexico next time. We didn't change our plans.

By Christmas, Abuelo was very sick. Within the first week of the new year, he died. I was devastated for my husband, but mostly I was racked with guilt. Why hadn't I insisted we change our plans? He'd only met Pacifique once when she was a baby. He'd never met little Claude. My heart ached for his loss and with the regret I knew my husband and I both felt for denying Abuelo something that would have brought him such joy.

As a mother, I longed to be able to say to Claude, "You may not remember him, but your Abuelo held you. I made sure you got to meet him." But I would never be able to say that. It was too late.

His loss and our distance from Mexico had reignited a desire to ensure my girls were connected with their Mexican heritage and their ancestors—hence our Day of the Dead altar and the famous photo of Abuelo—and that brings me to that moment I shared with Claude while we were packing up boxes.

To hell with "to-do" lists. These are the moments that count. I had Claude open the case and pass me the CD inside. She fetched the portable player, and I popped in the disk. She pressed play and, as she crawled into my lap, I wrapped my arms around her the way her grandfather would have. Her sobs subsided as she clutched the case close to her heart, and we swayed to "Abuelo's music."

Claude may not have met her Mexican grandfather, but for the time being, I can play Bocelli's music for her. And although she doesn't have a picture of herself in his arms like her sister does, when the first notes of *Angels We Have Heard on High* ring out, she believes her grandfather is singing to her. When the music plays, her smile lights up the room. It helps us all remember

Abuelo; it keeps his memory alive and singing.

Yes, living abroad comes at a price, but it has given us opportunities we couldn't have dreamed of back home. It has allowed us to spend more and better-quality time together as a family thanks to the generous holidays. It exposes the girls to different worlds, different cultures, different foods, and different ways of thinking. They speak three languages and a smattering of a few others.

Most importantly to us, they are unfazed by bindis or burkas. Rather than fearing difference, they embrace and welcome it. No matter where my girls end up, I trust they will march forth, meeting new people with the same warm, generous smile and wisdom as their Abuelo.

Long Distance Love

For moms who live far away.

You'll need:

1 oz. tequila
1 oz. orange liqueur
1 oz. orange juice
½ oz. sparkling water.
½ oz. fresh lime juice
A slice of lime or orange, for garnish

Method:

1. Fill a metal shaker with ice and add the ingredients (except the sparkling water).
2. Shake it like a pro and sieve into a souvenir martini glass from the airport gift shop.
3. Top with a splash of sparkling water.
4. Garnish with a slice of orange or lime, put on the music that makes you feel connected to your loved ones, and enjoy.

Toast to family, the music that connects us, and the memories that sing in our hearts.

The Wonder Part of Wonderful

Lynn Morrison

Have you ever noticed that when a TV character gives birth, one of the first things the doctor says to her is, "… and he has 10 perfect little fingers and 10 perfect little toes"? Then the TV mom swoons with delight and clutches her rather well-fleshed and not in the least squish-faced newborn child against her breast.

Having watched far too many "giving birth" movies in the last week of my pregnancy, I walked into the delivery room fully expecting the same experience. As I settled into my hospital bed, my husband snooped around the room, pointing out the plastic bassinet that would serve as a crib, the scale where our baby would be weighed, and all of the blank forms just waiting for a name, sex, and time of birth.

In between contractions, I reviewed his list of responsibilities. "You are here for me until she comes out. Then you are here for her. You've got to cut the cord, make sure that everything is perfect, and since I cannot get out of this bed, you have to make sure that I know that everything is perfect too." He nodded his head in understanding, and I tried to ignore that giant zit that was emerging on his chin (a sure indicator of his stress level).

Yet when the moment of truth came, despite my detailed instructions and the indications of his understanding, it was clear right away that neither my doctor nor my husband got my "made for TV birth" memo. Strapped into the bed by IV tubes and heart rate monitor cords, unable to see more than my legs hanging in mid-air, I started to get a bit frantic when everyone forgot about me.

"Does she have all her fingers and her toes?" I shouted across the delivery room. My husband stared at me with a blank look on his face. He had turned his brain to "off" when his wife pushed a baby out of her body.

"Does… she… have… ten… fingers… and… toes?" I asked again, carefully enunciating each word in the hopes that somehow I'd break through to him.

"Oh my god, I don't know," he responded, "I didn't look!" He jumped into action, trying to peer over the shoulders of the nurse who was weighing the baby. The woman caught sight of the crater that had formed on my husband's face, the angst on my own, and swooped our baby from the scale straight into my arms.

When I finally held my precious baby close, I stared down in wonder at her little fingers. They looked like they belonged on the hands of the Pillsbury Doughboy's love child—so chubby that the knuckles were nearly obscured—but there were ten of them, just as there should be. They were wonderful, and they were all mine.

Over the years, my daughter has grown. Her little wisps of hair turned into flowing locks. Knees and cheekbones emerged out of the pudgy baby fat. Her long torso and limber legs shot her up into girlhood. The only features that had been left recognizable from the tiny baby she once was were those chubby fingers.

I snuck into her room some nights and stared down at her in wonder. *How could I create such a perfect human? And, what can I place on top of her head to keep her from growing up any further?* I retrieved her stuffed monkey from the floor and placed it back under her arm, wiped the drool from her barely-chubby cheek, and pulled the covers up to keep her warm.

Each time her hands reached out to me for help, clutching tightly around my own slender digits, I could pretend for just a bit longer that she was still my little baby, despite all of the other evidence to the contrary. I can't postpone the inevitable transition into girlhood. I can't put the brakes on adolescence and the teenage years. But she will always be my baby, and she always will be wonderful.

And that brings us to today. Tonight at dinner, my five-and-a-half-year-old baby cleared her throat and made an announcement. She sat up straight in her chair, flipped her long blonde hair over her shoulder, smoothed the skirt of her school uniform over her long legs, and then waved her hand in the air to capture our attention.

"Mommy, Papa, look! I have a loose tooth!"

She folded down her fingers until only one remained—an unimaginably long and skinny index finger with a well-defined knuckle—and used its white-tipped fingernail to reach into her mouth and wiggle around her tooth.

I feigned a cough to choke back the tears and made all of the appropriate noises. She chattered on about tooth fairies and rewards. I pretended to swallow water down the wrong way to explain the tears in my eyes. She outlined all the things she would buy with her tooth fairy money, and I wondered where I could buy back her babyhood.

When she finally laid her head down upon her pillow, I smoothed her hair back from her forehead and looked desperately for some trace of the tiny infant I once knew.

As I stared at her in wonder, my beautiful woman-child daughter reached out her no-longer-chubby hand and brushed her fingers down my cheek. "I love you, Mommy. Will you read me a story?"

A loose tooth wiggled by an oh-so-grown-up finger made me cry for the loss of the sweet baby times she's left behind. With loving words and a caress from long fingers, my growing daughter wiped my tears away.

It turns out that my newborn baby isn't gone. She is merely hidden behind the glowing light of my bright, young girl who has just as much need for me as ever before. I can't help but wonder what she will do next. I know that whatever it is, it will certainly be wonderful.

The Verklempt

For moms who've got something in their eye.

You'll need:

1 ½ oz. vodka
1 ½ oz. lemon liqueur
1 oz. sweet and sour mix
1 tsp. sugar
1 oz. fresh lemon juice
A pinch of dried rosemary
A lemon slice, for garnish

Method:

1. Fill a metal shaker with ice and add all of the above ingredients.
2. Shake, weep, shake and strain into your martini glass of choice.
3. Garnish with a slice of lemon, wipe away your tears, and enjoy.

Toast to chubby hands, loose teeth, and the wonder moments that make us cry.

Tales of Woe

These tales are written by some funny moms who know, when it comes to parenthood, things don't always go as planned. Each relatable story speaks of survival and resilience and is followed by a simple-to-make martini and toast for you to share (in a victorious way) with your mom pals because we've all been there and we *love* to laugh about it.

When Family Fun Fails

Kate Parlin

Sometimes, as a parent, you have to give up. You have to know when to cut your losses, throw in the towel, and quit while you're ahead. There are a thousand clichés for this kind of thing because parents have been doing it for thousands of years. (I'm guessing, anyway. Kids probably gave their parents a hard time in ancient Greece, right?) And you know what happens when you fight it? Failure, crushed hopes, and day-drinking, that's what. I know because it happened to me.

I probably should have given up when I first realized the absurdity of my situation: I was a grown woman, all by myself in a petting zoo barn, feeding foul-smelling pellets to a bunch of crazy goats. There was no way this day was going to end well. I should have gathered the troops and taken them home to slump on the couch and read *The Very Hungry Caterpillar* for the millionth time, which is most likely all my children really wanted anyway. But I didn't, because goddamn it, it was Saturday. It was early fall, and the sun was shining. It was time to have some good old-fashioned family fun!

Earlier that day, my husband and I loaded our kids—two-year-old twins and a ten-month-old baby—into the wagon and stroller and headed to the County Fair. We imagined a delightful day of petting farm animals, eating fried food, and riding a carousel. This was going to be FUN. The pouty little faces beneath Minnie Mouse sunglasses suggested otherwise, but I ignored that. It would be so much FUN when we got there! Hooray for FAMILY FUN!

We went to the petting zoo barn first. From my kids' reaction *at the doorway of the barn*, you would have thought that the pens were filled with those enormous, nightmarish spiders from *The Hobbit* instead of sweet lil' baby animals.

They freaked. The. Hell. Out.

I looked around frantically for something to distract or entice my shrieking offspring. They were making a ridiculous scene. All I saw was a man (who looked like he was born without a sense of humor) perched on a stool by the goat pen. He was selling ice cream cones filled with food pellets for the animals. The goats acted like they hadn't eaten in months and would happily trample one another to death for a taste of those pellets. I thought maybe if I bought some of the stupid pellets and fed them to the stupid goats, the girls would feel more comfortable and want to try it themselves.

It didn't work.

Of course it didn't. I must have momentarily lost my head and forgotten that I wasn't dealing with reasonable people; I was dealing with two-year-olds. They kept on freaking out and begged to be taken out of the cool, dark barn and into the dust and merciless sun.

I was left feeding goats. By myself. Like a weirdo.

Ah, parenting.

After I had given away all of my pellets (ignoring the dark stare of Grouchy Pellet Man), my husband and I decided that we deserved some fair fries. It took a crazy amount of bribing and deal-making to get my grumpy toddlers *just to move their bodies in the direction of a fry vendor's booth*. They wouldn't ride in the wagon anymore. That wagon tried to wheel them right up into the Scary Barn of Death, so it was obviously not to be trusted.

We made our way to the fry booth only because one child got to pull the wagon (So. Painfully. Slowly.) and we promised to buy them balloons. I mean, that's a thing, right? I seem to remember getting balloons at the fair when I was a kid. Turns out that now, instead of balloons, they sell cheapo stuffed animals that are all displayed at two-year-old eye-level. They had balloons too, but not *normal* balloons. All we saw were horrible, misshapen unicorns and giant Spiderman thingies. Quite frankly, they looked more like blow-up dolls for fetishists than balloons for children. So we had to buy gross, overpriced stuffed animals from a swindler. I tried not to think about it too much when one of the girls cuddled her dusty, fake Care Bear up to her face.

We eventually ate fries, but they weren't as satisfying as I thought they'd be. Even covered in salt and vinegar, they tasted a little like crushed hopes. Oh and dust. Did I mention the dust? The girls liked the fries though, so I was hopeful that, with tummies full of tasty junk food, they would cheer up and have fun on the carousel.

When will I ever learn?

Our friends (who have *regular* kids who *like* baby animals and fair rides) met us there. They popped their little darlings up onto the painted ponies. My husband and I talked up the carousel like it was damn Disney World, but the girls weren't having any of it. They refused to get on. As the cheerful music played, we stood there like idiots, waving to our friends' kids every time they came around while our own daughters glared sullenly at a trash can.

Sigh.

That was it. I was done. I wanted to check out the displays of enormous pumpkins. I wanted to eat a huge plate of fried dough covered in sugar. I wanted to buy homemade soap from some earnest-looking beekeepers or *something*. But more than any of those things, I wanted to get away from my scowling little fun-suckers. In order to do that, we had to leave the fair behind, take the girls home, and pray that they would go down for a nap. Surely they must be tired, right? RIGHT?

Instead, when we got home, they said, "Mommy, we want to do finger painting."

They insisted. They would not agree to watch *Daniel Tiger*, to read a book, or to take a nap.

Really? REALLY?!? After schlepping around in the hot sun and dust with a pair of cranky two-year-olds, I now had to supervise FINGER PAINTING?!?

I finally accepted defeat. What choice did I have? I put them in my old t-shirts and let them make a giant mess. Then I did the only logical thing any frazzled parent can do at that point: I pulled the vodka out of the freezer and rummaged around in the fridge for something—really, anything at all—to use as a mixer. I found one of those strawberry margarita-in-a-bottle thingies and thought, why not? What else can you do when your hopes for a day of family fun have been so thoroughly squashed by two diapered dictators?

So, fellow parents-in-arms, I learned something that day: sometimes it's best for everyone if you just give up. Family fun is overrated. Take a rest, have a drink, and remember that there's always next year.

Strawberry Margatini

For moms who keep planning the outings, optimistic that family fun is within reach, even though they should know better.

You'll need:

1 ½ oz. tequila
1 ½ oz. pureed strawberries
1 oz. lemonade
A strawberry or slice of lime, for garnish

Method:

1. Fill a metal shaker with ice and add the above ingredients.
2. Shake that shaker, while doing a tired-mom version of *The Macarena*.
3. Strain this tasty blend into your martini glass of choice and enjoy. A side of Fair Fries optional.

Toast to fairs, fries, and failed family fun.

And, Brace Yourself…

Shannon Day

Don't you just love how motherhood completely redefines the act of getting ready for a night out? No longer is it a process involving the leisurely sipping of vino while carefully selecting an outfit. Gone are the days of uninterrupted showers complete with full grooming time, tools and products at the ready.

Remember those days, ladies? They were good, weren't they? We were preened and pruned, from toes to eyebrows and everywhere in between. If only we'd known to savour those moments more when we had all that endless time, freedom, and peace.

Unappreciated luxury. That's what that was.

These days, we're lucky to snag a night out in the first place; with the fate of our freedom held tightly in the hands of a teenage babysitter. And then when the evening of the event comes, we're often left with but a quick window in which to get ready. From shower to outfit, we are experts at the 15-minute makeover. Well maybe we're not total experts yet, but we're working on it—one half-shaven leg at a time.

On one particular evening, I decided that I wasn't going to settle for a 15-minute window. My husband was dishing up dinner for the kids, and the plan was to put on a movie afterwards. The conditions were ideal, really. And with over an hour before the babysitter was set to arrive, I knew what I had to do: I poured myself a glass of wine and I sashayed my way up the stairs, feeling both hopeful and a tad giddy.

I turned on the bath and started browsing through my closet. I perused through my dresses and contemplated wearing one of them. I decided on a sparkly top and some skinny jeans instead so I could wear my semi-comfy ankle boots. Happy with my choices, I laid everything out on the bed, picked out some jewelry and a handbag, and then headed back to the bathroom, locking the door behind me.

My steamy bubble bath beckoned...

I dimmed the lights, stripped off my clothes, and—wine in hand—embarked upon a mini-adventure. Well, it felt like one anyway. What an indulgence! Just me, my wine, my...

RAP RAP RAP! went the door.

"Mommy!" said the little voice on the other side of it.

Grrrrrrr, I grumbled to myself. "I'm just having a bath. I'll be out soon!"

I thought they were watching a movie.

"Mom? What's going on? Why is the door locked?"

All three girls were now gathered outside the bathroom door.

Sigh.

BANG BANG BANG! went the door.

"I'm just in the bath!" I shouted. "Can I please have—"

The door flung open.

WTF?!

A coin had been used to pick the lock, and the girls

piled in, giggling, proud of their clever break-in. Within seconds, little clothes were scattered across the bathroom floor and three naked bodies had joined me in the bath. Just like that, my peaceful and serene environment had been replaced with overcrowded conditions and excessive noise. I fumbled my way out of the tub, surrendering it over to the kids.

My mini-adventure was over. But, it wasn't long before my furrowed brow softened to the sounds of hysterical laughter at crazy bubble beards and fluffy white hairdos.

They *were* pretty cute, but I was no further ahead, so I hopped into the shower for some half-assed grooming and a quick wash. I then threw on my robe and got all the kids dried off and into their PJs.

By that point, 45 minutes had flown by and I was now on the 15-minute countdown.

I furiously blow-dried my hair, slapped on some make-up, earrings, and my sparkly top. I then shimmied into my jeans and stopped for a quick glance in the mirror. "Not bad" I said to myself, surprised. "Not bad at all."

I then leaned over to put on my boots.

Almost ready.

"Aaaaaachoooo!" I sneezed. And… I peed.

It wasn't a massive pee, but it was a pee. A sneeze-pee.

But, I wouldn't be referring to myself as "Pissy-Pants" just yet, nor would I get my knickers in a twist about it. There was no time for that. Instead, I simply changed my underwear, shimmied back into my unscathed jeans and boots, and with a reaffirming glance in the mirror, I was ready to hit the town.

When the doorbell rang, I walked my imaginary catwalk down the hallway to greet the babysitter.

Getting ready for a night out certainly isn't what it

used to be, and neither are my pelvic floor muscles. But hey, such is the life of a mom—a mom who clearly needs to do more Kegels.

The Pelvic Floor

For moms who need to do more Kegels.

You'll need:

1 ½ oz. vodka
1 ½ oz. lemonade
¾ oz. raspberry liqueur
Fresh mint leaves, for garnish.

Method:

1. Fill a metal shaker with ice and add the above ingredients
2. Shake your booty and the shaker.
3. Strain your Pelvic Floor into a martini glass (you won't learn *that* in yoga class).
4. Garnish with mint and do a Kegel with every sip. (New drinking game? Oh yes it is.)

Toast to peace-free baths, to imaginary catwalks, and to knowing when to brace yourself.

"Seesh"—a Love(y) Story

Jen Dean

"Where's Seesh?"

I froze, every nerve suddenly alive and crackling with panic. My mouth went dry and it felt like a bowling ball had dropped through my lower intestine. I became aware of a low moaning noise and realized it was coming from me.

"Nooooooooooooooooooo," I was whimpering.

You would think this short, silly sentence uttered by a preschooler would be a harmless one. You would be wrong. Those two little words have the ability to make our entire household come to a screeching, paralyzed halt. Bad shit is about to go down—DEFCON One, Threat Level: Red, B.A.D. Bad.

"Who is Seesh?" you ask? Seesh is a stuffed dolphin whose name, incidentally, comes from a toddler's mispronunciation of FISH. But he is no ordinary stuffed dolphin. He is my middle son's "lovey." With Buzz Lightyear as my witness, I swear there hasn't been a more powerful bond between boy and toy since Andy and Woody.

You don't truly grasp the magnitude of this unconditional love until you've had a child and they've had a treasured item. When parents speak about their child's "lovey," moms and dads from all walks of life with kids of all ages will immediately give them a knowing nod. They will probably even launch into their own lovey story, because all parents seem to have a lovey story.

I still remember a good friend calling frantically from the Las Vegas Airport over a decade ago. Her two-year-old had lost the Pooh-Bear blankie that I'd given her and was inconsolable. Since this was the pre-Amazon age, she was desperate to find a way to replace it. I didn't have children yet, but the sobbing that I could hear (from both mother and daughter) through the phone hurtled me into action.

I'd raced back to the baby store and explained the dilemma to the store clerk, a grandma who totally "got it." She called three other stores before we could find an exact replica that she immediately had shipped. It wasn't the original, and the toddler knew it, but she begrudgingly accepted her consolation prize.

My middle son, however, would not—and will not ever—accept a consolation prize. Seesh is Seesh. Period. How do I know? Oh, how we've tried. My favourite example is when a babysitter once bought him the exact same dolphin in a sweet but misguided attempt to have a backup in place.

"Where's Seesh?" he asked.

"Right here!" she said brightly as she handed him the new dolphin.

He took one look at the replacement and scoffed. I didn't even know it was possible for a three-year-old to scoff.

"That's not Seesh!" he giggled. "This one is all… fluffy." He sniffed it and made a face while firmly shaking his head no.

"I washed him!" She gamely gave it a second shot.

"No. This isn't Seesh. I need Seesh." He had crossed over from amused to annoyed and was rapidly approaching pissed.

I observed this whole exchange from a few steps away with Seesh behind my back. I could see where this was headed and swooped in to end the charade.

So when we hear "Where's Seesh?" at bedtime, inevitably alarm bells go off. Seesh has become an irreplaceable touchstone for an anxious, internal little guy who sometimes feels stuck in the middle. Seesh offers comfort, security, and unconditional love to my son, a boy who has a hard time accepting those things from others.

Every time I hear that dreaded phrase, I flash through millions of possible scenarios in a nanosecond. Did we leave him at a store? Was he outside being eaten by a raccoon? Was he stuck between the seats of the minivan? Did the big brother hide him again? (Not if he wants to see his next birthday, the little shit.) Maybe the baby waddled off with him? Seesh has wound up in so many different hiding places that we've suffered without him on more than one occasion.

The longest heart-wrenching stretch lasted three days. "Missing" posters were created; Facebook statuses were updated; friends, neighbors, and sitters were all recruited to help search. I eventually found Seesh buried in a washer load of towels. My son, despite his distress, had never lost faith that Seesh would return. He simply gave him a big hug and said: "Wow, good hiding place Seesh. Let's not play that game again." And then he wandered off, Seesh firmly in tow. I found myself randomly sobbing with relief on and off for hours.

This time, though, we were about to trump all "missing Seesh" stories because this time we were on a beach vacation. As usual, it was bedtime, so it was dark out, meaning if Seesh wasn't in the condo, it could get ugly. Predictably, the condo and car were ransacked to the point of looking like crime scenes—but, no Seesh.

My husband looked at me pityingly as I grabbed a flashlight and insisted on at least checking the pool area and boardwalk. We both knew I wasn't going to find Seesh out there. I'd find malaria, maybe, since the mosquitos were in full attack mode, but no way was I going to find a sad and dirty, little, stuffed dolphin.

I lay awake all night running through our day, trying to figure out when and where we'd last seen Seesh. My son insisted he'd never taken him out of his room, so he was no help. Just as I was dozing off, it came to me.

I bolted upright.

Oh my God, he's right. He didn't take Seesh out of his room—I did! On the way to a new restaurant for lunch, I had grabbed Seesh and thrown him in my bag because I knew that new restaurants, with their strange menus, could be stressful.

Holy crap. I lost Seesh. I'll take "Mommy Guilt" for $2,000, Alex.

Then I really couldn't sleep because I desperately needed to call the restaurant and see if someone had found Seesh. "Please," I prayed to every deity that I thought might listen. "Please keep him safe. Please let him be there."

When I was finally able to call the *Lazy Flamingo* and ask if anyone had found a very well-loved stuffed dolphin, the manager who answered sounded just as relieved and excited as I felt when he said, "Yes!"

He continued, "We could tell how much this little guy was loved. We were so worried about him. He's on display on top of the bar with all of the stuffed flamingos because we hoped he'd be recognized from up there."

When we got to the restaurant to collect Seesh,

almost the entire staff came up to greet us. I could tell they were as overjoyed by the reunion as we were. The manager leaned down to speak to my son. He told him Seesh had enjoyed a fantastic adventure with the flamingos and made new friends for life. He said they'd love to have him back to visit any time. He even gave us some souvenirs to remember them by. Their kindness was so overwhelming that my son and I both had to go back outside and take a minute to compose ourselves.

"Seesh is unstoppable," my husband chuckled later in hushed awe.

"It puts a whole new twist on those *Toy Story* movies, doesn't it?" I laughed.

I glanced back at Seesh, who looked quite content as he nestled in my son's arms. I swear he winked at me.

The James Bond

For mission-minded moms who save the day.

You'll need:

1 oz. vodka
1 white sugar cube
2 dashes of citrus bitters
2 oz. chilled champagne

Method:

1. Fill a metal shaker with ice, add the vodka, and shake it up.
2. Drop a sugar cube into a classic martini glass, moisten with citrus bitters.
3. Strain the vodka into your glass and top with champagne.
4. Give it a gentle, barely there, stir because we like our post-mission martinis shaken *and* stirred.

Toast to the bond between mother and child, the bond between child and lovey, and to our James Bond-worthy missions that save the day.

Double Trouble

Tara Wilson

Me: "Let's get pet bunnies. They'll be fluffy and adorable, and with two of them they can keep each other company while we're at work. Plus there will be one for each of us to snuggle so we won't need to have a tug of war, and accidentally pull off its ears."

Husband: "I don't think you should own *any* animals, let alone multiples."

Me: "But it will be great! I've read that you can litter train them, and they're quiet, which is perfect for apartment pets! Puhllleeeeeeaaaaasssssseeeee??????"

Husband: "All right, let's get two rabbits! What could go wrong?"

Cue ominous soundtrack.

I think we must have been high from the smoke wafting up from the drug-dealing neighbours who lived below us. That or we thought fluffy animals would be an effective distraction from the *Wanted for Murder* posters hanging in the stairwell.

I believe we could have handled *one* rabbit. Or maybe just a *photo* of a rabbit. Sure, the rabbit-training handbook has a long section on how to litter train your snuggly bunny by gently picking her up and placing her in the litter box whenever she has an accident. What the book does *not* cover, however, is that it's impossible to tell which lop-eared monster shit on the rug when you have more than one offender. Do you *know* how much poop comes out of *one* rabbit, let alone *two*? I'm convinced this is where the term *crapload* originated.

The handbook also fails to mention what to do when the rabbits eat the book—a bunny's equivalent of laughing in our faces, because rabbits can't actually laugh, and shitting in my lap didn't send a strong enough message. Sure they were adorable, we loved them, and they enjoyed having each other for company. But together they worked as a team to destroy our entire apartment. I swore I would never bring home TWO of something ever again.

Fast-forward a few years to the examining room of the lab where I was having an ultrasound. I was dangerously close to breaking toileting convention myself, with an overfull bladder and a technician-in-training. Just when I thought we were in the home stretch she announced that her supervisor would have to verify her work. I suggested that she gather the janitor as long as she was sending out invitations, because shit was about to get real.

I was so focussed on clenching and thinking about the aridness of deserts that I almost missed the part when she said, "Here is the heartbeat... aaaannnnd over *here* is *another* little bunny..."

WHAT?!?

She sure as hell better be talking about our one-year-old who's sitting in my husband's lap. Or that an actual bunny has gotten loose in the room. Surely it's one of those things. It will be okay. I'm not going to have three children under two.

Phew, dodged a bullet there.

Wait a minute, why are they talking about twins? And why is my husband smiling like that? One of us must be having a stroke. If it's me, then I am definitely going to pee on this table.

In the end they were finally able to convey to me that I really was carrying twins, and that the ultrasound tech didn't receive her training through the mail. The people in the waiting room stared at us as I staggered by, looking like a mole woman emerging from underground, while my husband appeared to have drunk seven espressos and seen a unicorn.

Once the initial shock wore off, I too decided that this was fantastic news. Molly had been such an easy baby, so how much harder could it be to have two at once, especially now that we were seasoned professionals? (More of those delusions from the bunny days, only this time we didn't even have a pot-smoking neighbour to blame.)

Most of my pregnancy was uneventful, and in some ways I felt better than with the first one. Of course, I needed Big Bird and Cookie Monster to raise my toddler because I couldn't move, and I couldn't fit into an average-sized powder room, let alone my maternity clothes. Just as I contemplated stealing the parachute from Molly's gymnastics class to wear as a shirt, the babies decided they were ready to pull the ripcord.

I delivered the twins within half an hour of arriving at the hospital. Not because I was too busy eating ice cream or because my husband couldn't find his keys (miraculously), but because the babies were already showing me that they would always keep me on my toes—when I wasn't on my back screaming, that is. There was no time for an epidural, so believe me, there was screaming.

Delivering a baby without pain meds once is hard, but manageable. Being told to do it all over again five minutes later is a form of torture the military may want to consider if they are looking to up their game. That was just the first of many times I would learn that all the hard parts of having a baby were doubled with twins. I always was pretty good at math.

The early months were brutal. That may even be sugar-coating it. Maggie and Grace both had colic and would scream for hours at a time, unable to be soothed. I'm not sure if it was worse when they screamed one at a time, threatening the silence of her rarely-slumbering sister, or when they did it in tandem so that I had a child deafening both ears at once, like hysterical headphones without volume control.

I thought I would never make it through those early months. In fact I wasn't sure *they* would make it if I kept taking the wrong baby in to the doctor's office. (They're not even identical twins!) I was one step away from bringing a random kid from the lobby into the examining room.

We did eventually come out the other side of colic and sleeping in shifts, and Maggie and Grace slept in a bedroom together, in side-by-side cribs. When I say *slept*, I mean jumped furiously up and down like they were at an all-night baby rave. The cribs didn't last for long either. Grace started climbing from her crib into Maggie's crib at sixteen months. And that's when we made a monumental error *for safety*—we dismantled the cribs and moved their mattresses to the floor. The inmates were free and there was rioting to be done.

I once walked in on Maggie standing in the middle drawer of the dresser while Grace prepared to shove it closed. Every naptime I would find the room destroyed, with all their clothes strewn about. And just like with the rabbits, I didn't know which of them to put in the litter box.

As they got their walking legs they ran in opposite directions at every opportunity, and I had to chase whichever one was running toward the scariest thing. Unless it was a spider. If you're running toward a spider… you're on your own.

I thought I'd outsmarted them by outfitting them with those backpack leashes. I decided to test them out, one day, by taking the twins for a walk around the block. It was ridiculously easy and I patted myself on the back for getting something right for a change. We walked along in that pleasant "we could walk faster in quicksand because everything is fascinating" way that toddlers do. Life was good. Until we rounded the corner and it all went to *shit*.

One twin started bolting for home. The other was steadfast in her "no looking back" position and tried to stretch on ahead. At some point they doubled-back and I found myself hogtied from the leashes they had wound around my legs. That's when the first twin sat down, staging a political sit-in about the rights to boob and arrowroot cookies. I had one kid who would only move forward and one refusing to move *anywhere* on her own at this point, but screaming if I carried her any further away from the house, even though we were walking in a damn circle.

It was clear to me what had to be done. I picked them both up under my arms, football style, and started to run. Football players really don't realize how easy they have it, only having to carry one small football, not two large screaming toddlers wearing horsey backpacks. And at least the players get to wear padding and a cup. My yoga pants were no match for the writhing anger of the twins kicking me in the crotch.

The expression *Double Trouble* exists for a reason. And at times I felt like the trouble was more exponential than doubled. The feeding and changing schedules required a spreadsheet more complicated than the flight plan at an international airport, we were drowning in laundry and dishes, our triple stroller was larger than a Smart Car, and I never felt like I had enough arms.

But none of that mattered. All of the good parts of having twins far outweigh the hair-tearing bits. I needed more arms because mine were full of three children who have brought more joy to my life than I ever could have imagined. Full arms is a pretty great problem to have, I'd say.

Much better than a lap full of rabbit poop.

The Fab ~~Pair~~ Pear

For moms of twins.

You'll need:

1 ½ oz. vanilla vodka
½ oz. orange liqueur
2 oz. natural pear juice
A slice of pear, for garnish

Method:

1. Fill a metal shaker with ice and add the above ingredients.
2. Shake, shake, shake and strain into your martini glass.
3. Garnish with a slice of pear (or two) and enjoy.
4. Keep track of your drink in case it looks like someone else's.

Toast to happy surprises, the adventure of raising twins, and the joy of having arms full of love.

French Women Don't Get Fat

Vicki Lesage

French women really *are* skinnier. Even when pregnant.

Those *pouffiasses*! Which, by the way, is the most hilarious word. You're trying to call them the b-word and you end up saying "poufy-ass." Too bad it isn't closer to the truth. They have perfectly shaped butts, as perfect as the delicious *pain au chocolat* I stuff in my mouth. You'll never spot one of them with a muffin-top. Mmm, muffins.

I think I discovered my problem. Maybe if I wasn't so busy gorging myself on croissants filled with chocolate and calling people names (and comparing derrieres to pastries), I'd be svelte like them.

Or not.

Looking at a typical day in the life of this American in Paris, I realize it's hopeless from the start. It's hard enough trying to act chic in such a cosmopolitan capital without getting a heel stuck in cobblestone or stepping in one of the numerous piles of dog poop. I barely manage to twist a scarf around my neck in the effortlessly posh way Parisians do, and when I do succeed, it takes me at least 15 minutes and multiple swear words.

So, yes, my compatriots will always look better than me. My ass will always be bigger than theirs. And let's not even *talk* about my pregnant ass.

Except, let's do. During my first pregnancy, I was pretty active—for my own health and also to avoid standing out even more as an enormous whale in a sea of supermodels. Glancing around the waiting room at my prenatal check-ups, I was the only one harboring a watermelon; the other pregnant ladies, even those who were months closer to their due date, were incubating a cantaloupe at best. If anyone asked, I'd say I was due the next day—not the next season.

I made it through those appointments by ignoring the gorgeous women around me and dreaming of the treat I'd pick up at the *patisserie* on the way home. My impossibly thin French husband never complained about my increasing proportions; he's the one that brought the pastries home half the time.

Then, before I could gorge on any more buttery, flaky goodness, my 7 ½ -pound preemie made his arrival. He was a huge bundle of joy—if a bit earlier than planned. Imagine how much he would have weighed if he'd made it to term!

The one bright side of my son being born early—literally, the one aspect that didn't bring me to tears—was that I had a mere eight months of pregnancy weight to shed. I'm scared to think how much I would have gained in that last month! *(Quick calculation: 2 croissants x 30 days x a whole lotta calories = lots of extra jiggle in my wiggle)*

My son was released from the NICU after 11 long days with a clean bill of health. We began our new life together of sleepless nights, tired days, and nonstop nursing. Somehow, after a few months, I returned to my original size. I'm guessing it had to do with my low-calorie, high-exercise diet: I often forgot to eat and was constantly running around trying to stay on top of laundry and doctor's appointments and more laundry.

At that point, a French woman would still drown in my clothes. But that was as good as it was gonna get for this North American mama.

Then, right as summer was ending and I'd gotten used to showing off my toned arms in my stylish sleeveless tops, I got pregnant with my daughter. Goodbye skinny jeans, hello muumuus!

Any plans I had to not gain as much weight this time around were thwarted when I was put on bed rest at 5 ½ months. I spent the next 14 weeks on the couch, eating quiche, gaining weight, and keeping my baby girl safe and snug until almost full-term.

Totally worth it.

A few weeks after my daughter was born, our neighbors had a baby girl as well. A few weeks after *that*, the mother was back to her pre-pregnancy weight… which was about 30 pounds skinnier than I could ever hope to be, even on the best of diets. It's possible my *newborn daughter* weighed more than this beanpole of a woman (I wanted to say "stripper pole" but I've already called French women bitches. I should probably be nicer. But it's not fair!!!!!! *stuffs tarte aux pommes into whining mouth*).

What was I saying?

Adding insult to injury, we live across the street from a maternity hospital. From the comfort of my apartment, clad in stretchy Size L yoga pants that would never be used for yoga, I could see impossibly thin women leave the hospital with their tiny bundles of joy in their skinny little arms.

Pouffiasses.

But being jealous wasn't doing me any good. Life isn't fair, and we all know it. I needed to stop complaining and to start doing something about it. So I packed up the pastries and unpacked Zumba for Wii. I stomped around my apartment like a drunken rhinoceros, hopelessly out of sync to the music, but burning calories nonetheless. My son joined in with embarrassingly more rhythm than me. My daughter watched with a huge, supportive grin on her angelic face. It was… dare I say… FUN.

My daughter is almost nine months old now. I'm happily down to Size M in yoga pants, though I still have no plans to actually use them for yoga. I've got a little junk in my trunk, but if I wear the right clothes, no one has to know.

I may never be as skinny as these French *femmes*, but I don't have to be. I have two wonderful kids and an adoring husband who loves me the way I am. I'm healthy, if not perfectly thin. My big, American bones are doing just fine.

We can toast to that, right?

The Skinny French

For moms who embrace le junk in le trunk.

You'll need:

2 oz. vodka
¾ oz. raspberry liqueur
1 ½ oz. light pineapple juice

Method:

1. Fill a metal shaker with ice and add the above ingredients.
2. Shake it up, knowing that this may very well be the best martini you've ever tasted, and strain into a lovely martini glass.
3. Sip this frothy deliciousness while wearing your (mandatory) yoga pants and (optional) beret.

Toast to France, rants, and fitting into your pants.

When the Shit Hits the ~~Fan~~ Wall

Tamara Schroeder

Before I had kids, I wrongly assumed that the time I woke up in the middle of the night to the sound of our dog gagging would be the grossest thing I would ever have to deal with. On that occasion, my husband yelled at him not to throw up on the bed, so the dog leaned over the edge and puked into a basket full of clean, folded laundry.

Having children was kind of like that—except my life was the basket of laundry, and I was woefully underprepared to be figuratively and literally puked on. I was also unprepared for being defecated on and having random body fluids wiped on me. At least when I got tired of the dog's crap (whether figuratively or literally), I could leave him home alone and escape the madness for a while. Child services frowns on temporary abandonment as a coping mechanism in parenting.

But nothing—*nothing*—could have prepared me for the shit that came with having kids. The actual, literal shit. Figurative shit is annoying, but it doesn't smell nearly as bad, nor does it stain your carpet.

When my child was two and a half, we decided to potty train him. For the sake of the (mostly) innocent, I will refer to the offender as "he/him" and will not confirm which of my children this story is about. The odds of guessing which of my kids it was in this case are 50/50, but no one deserves to be known, beyond the shadow of a doubt, as a turd-spreader for their whole life. People will just have to make gross assumptions about the turd-spreader's true identity. Good luck in college, kids. This is going to be a tough reputation for you to live down, and one of you doesn't even deserve it.

Toilet training during the awake-hours went fairly smoothly. Looking back now, I suspect it was probably worse than I remember. But what came after those early days was so horrifying that Guantanamo Bay seems a quiet, relaxing vacation with wait staff in comparison ... so I suppose it's all relative.

In any case, this particular child had dealt with constipation issues since babyhood, and as a result, he was terrified of pooping on the toilet. Instead, he would wait until naptime or bedtime when he was put in a Pull-Up and do his business in the training pants. By this time, he was used to wearing underwear for most of the day. Naturally (but unfortunately for us), he didn't particularly enjoy the sensation of feces on his skin. However, instead of calling us to change him, he would put his hands in his pants and scoop out what he could.

The even bigger problem (both for us and for him) was that he now had poop on his nether-regions and his hands. His response was to panic and wipe his hands everywhere. I wish that was hyperbole, but no space was too sacred. Walls, dresser drawers (and quite often the contents), the back of the door, the carpet, comforter and pillowcases were his canvas. It was like the worst kind of finger-painting you could possibly imagine. Except, I hadn't imagined it. Had I been able to, I probably wouldn't have played it so fast and loose with the idea of procreating.

In fact, when I asked a group of friends for advice and possible solutions, the discussion quickly devolved into the idea of creating a PSA for people considering parenthood, using my example as a reason to reconsider. Camaraderie was about the only thing anyone could offer me. Camaraderie and alcohol.

My vague memories of that time include wiping down surfaces with bleach (often multiple times a day), doing endless amounts of laundry, and sobbing. All these activities took place with a glass of wine never more than an arm's reach away (also often multiple times a day). Even once his room was spotless and the physical evidence was wiped clean, the smell—which I would liken to the devil's jock strap—lingered to humble me should I ever get too confident in my role as a parent.

I'm happy to say this child eventually outgrew that phase, and I learned some things along the way. Here is my advice:

1) Invest in the oversized bottles of vodka. The standard size disappears far too quickly. Then, not only are you cleaning and sanitizing all day, you're also saddled with the guilt of being on a first-name basis with the liquor store clerk, and even she's starting to shoot you judgmental looks. It's much more practical in terms of price and peace of mind to just buy the biggest one they have from the outset. Plus, if you run out of bleach, vodka makes a great disinfectant.

2) Sorry, that's all I've got.

I wish I could offer more helpful suggestions or tips for parents experiencing similar issues, but I've blocked most memories from that period. It's just one big, foggy, brown haze.

The Shit-Storm

For moms who are living a poop-filled existence.

You'll need:

1 oz. vanilla vodka
1 oz. hazelnut liqueur
1 oz. coffee liqueur
1 oz. cream
Shredded chocolate, to sprinkle on top

Method:

1. Wash your hands thoroughly and burn your clothes!
2. Fill a metal shaker with ice and the above ingredients.
3. Shake it up and strain into your martini glass of choice.
4. Sprinkle shredded chocolate on top, find a clean spot to sit, and enjoy.

Toast to stain-resistant surfaces, to all the shit-storms that parenting brings, and to making it through to the sweeter-smelling side.

The Popsicle Doesn't Fall Far From the Tree

Brooke Takhar

A snippet from a recent conversation with my 4 year old in the car:

> Stella (from the back seat): "Puh-puh-Pocky please?"
> *pause*
> "HEY. Pocky starts with a 'P' just like popsicle!"
> Me: "That's right!"
> *pause*
> Stella: "I DID MATH!"
> Me: "…"

Give me a hot second and I can still recall the exact day geometry was introduced in elementary school and the ensuing raging gut ache and light-headedness it created. Angles and formulas and *what now*? I was *just* out on the playground pretending to be the President of the Babysitter's Club and flinging ketchup packages at dirty-sneakered boys, and now you want me to be an engineer?

NO.

I would wander the room, peering over shoulders as my so-called friends quickly grasped the foreign concepts. They shouted with glee as they got the correct answers and twirled their protractors like tiny, pompous douchebags. I sat and stared at the mimeographed sheets with their dangerous dilemmas and just slowly sweated while drawing tiny broken hearts around the edge of the paper.

As the years passed, my constant C's in math did a fine job of yanking my GPA down.

At 16, I had a math teacher who was also a driver's ed instructor. He was the kind of confident, balding male that married another math teacher, who tucked his shirt into pleated pants, and who would tell us at least once a week, apropos of nothing, that every car accident could be avoided. I imagined his home life to be as square as the only shape I actually recognized in math class. I hated him. I hated how I felt in that class: trapped and dumb. I paid *so much* attention. I lasered holes through my handouts with intense intent. But it was all still Greek. The math had only gotten harder, and my brain was still 47 clumsy steps behind.

Not once over 11 long butt-clenching years, from first bell to last bell, did I *ever* consider asking for help from *any* teacher. A lot of those teachers liked me, and I considered them safe allies. They loved my short stories written first in painstakingly small penciled lines, then in blue cursive. I could have told them math made me ache, and I would have been directed to some help. I could have breathed and solved my math anxiety like a neatly clicked-into-place Rubik's Cube.

Not once in my entire school career did I ever greet my mom when she arrived home from work and ask *her* for some help. The woman I adored, emulated, and made dinner for so she could just kick off her heels with a clatter and sink down at the table—my hero—I never told that I needed help with this subject in school that had marked me with a Scarlet Letter: C for "Can't Math."

Somehow, some way, I passed all the necessary math courses needed to receive a high school diploma and then swiftly bought a calculator watch. Then came cell phones with calculators and Google access so that I would never again have to sweat numbers.

Big fat calendar years passed as I got married, got pregnant, tugged a kid out from between my legs, and now my Stella will start kindergarten in September. There is so much to be uncovered. Will her brain work like mine or her dad's? Will she be loud or shrink? Will she kick or be kicked? Tattle or understand the overarching lesson of *The Godfather* (snitches get stitches)? Have a comfortable grasp on numbers, or drown in the space between their sharp, judgy black and white edges?

I don't know. What I *do* know is I will encourage her to come to us with any problem, any question, or any confusion. I will do my very best to find an answer or someone who knows the answer. I will encourage her to never sit slumped in her desk and stew in her sadness or feelings of inadequacy. A) It gets stinky really quickly, and B) the answers are never found under your desk where you sadly etch out swear words instead of grasping what the fuck X is.

We'll fly in doctors, scientists, and a sliver of Hawking's brain matter. OR, we'll just Google it. Our home will be a haven where math comes to be solved. When the unsolvable becomes clear, I imagine it will taste as good as a popsicle on a hot summer's day. We'll buy a box of her favourites and split it 50/50—six for me and four for her. *MATH!*

The Creamsicle-tini

For mathematically challenged moms.

You'll need:

1 ½ oz. vanilla vodka
1 oz. orange liqueur
1 oz. orange juice
1 oz. orange soda
1 oz. cream
An orange sugar candy, for garnish

Method:

1. Fill a metal shaker with ice and add the above ingredients. Just eyeball it if measuring feels too much like math.
2. Give that shaker a mega-shake and then strain your beautiful mixture into your martini glass.
3. Garnish with an orange candy, make peace with your past mathematical woes, and enjoy.

Toast to X, to Y and to the parallelogram, even though we don't actually know what any of you are.

Who Needs a Facial?

Carolyn Mackenzie

At least once a month, my mom comes over to my house with some kind of beauty product for me to try. As usual I mutter, "Thanks, Mom," and tuck it away in my bathroom cupboard, alongside the last dozen little bottles and tubes that have come my way.

This week, she brought an all-natural cucumber and green tea face mask.

"You must try it! You'll glow afterwards!" she told me.

I mumbled something incoherent under my breath, and then I gave the tube a number and filed it away because, let's be honest, the only mask I can relate to these days is a superhero's. If it's not plastic, with eyes cut out and pointed ears, it's not in my life.

It's amazing how quickly I forget the good 'ol days when facial masks, or any kind of spa treatment, were not considered a novelty. They were just commonplace. If I wanted it, I did it. Plain and simple. Cut and dried. All body parts were given the kind of TLC I now give my children. From toes to brows, no body part felt neglected. And NEVER did I run out of a hair appointment with wet locks because a blow dry would make me late for the after school pick-up.

That was then, but this is now. And all those activities that I once took for granted are a rarity. A rarity that can only be experienced, to the utmost, if I'm as far away from the kids as possible—in a place where clocks, Pull-Ups, and lunch pails don't exist.

Admittedly, self-grooming has improved since the early years of child-rearing. My children are now three and six, which means it *is* possible to shave my legs on occasion. But if I look farther down, unless a vacation has been booked, my toes and their sad nails are in a deep depression. I suppose if I really tried, I could etch out some time to squeeze in a pedi, particularly on those days when I look at the laundry and kitchen and say, "Tomorrow… "

However, another problem arises when *the couch* beckons, "Coooomeeee heeerrrrree," and "siiiiiiitttttt doooowwwn." And at times like that, I simply can't resist. I savour those moments when I find myself alone with the couch and a quiet house. I turn on a made-for-TV movie, grab the chocolate almonds from the cupboard, and, at that moment, not even the promise of a pedi could tear me off that cushiony island of salvation.

Sorry, toes.

But aside from my couch (and the chocolate almonds), the real enemy here is the clock. I work from 4 p.m. until midnight, five nights a week, anchoring the 11 p.m. news for a local TV station. Now I have to admit, there is at least one built-in luxury that comes with my job: I don't apply my own make-up. I leave my house looking like Mom, and at work our make-up magician turns me into a person whom my kids have never met. But as our make-up artist, Dana, often reminds me, she works with brushes not wands. *Sigh.* If only…

Regardless, she works wonders and breathes life into my tired face. Even my poor, neglected eyebrows are reborn under her expert care. Another make-up artist once reminisced about a time, long past, when I'd walk in with perfectly shaped brows. He then sighed and pulled out his tweezers, quietly adding, "those were *BBK*." Brows Before Kids.

Each night (rather, morning), I arrive home at 1 a.m., check in on the kids, and dive into bed. I'm asleep five seconds later because I never know how long my eyes will stay shut. If, by some miracle, no one has a nightmare, wets the bed, or runs a fever, then sleep is my best friend until 7 a.m. on the nose, when my three-year-old sleep-enemy yells, "MOMMY!" He's so loud it makes me think the Avengers are in his room actively recruiting him for service.

My response time to my children's holler is wickedly impressive, by the way. I usually throw my neck or back out in this swift, yet not-so-spry, leap out of bed. It's odd that my husband, who IS a legitimate first responder, never actually responds in a quick fashion to ANYTHING in our home. I, on the other hand, no matter how tired, jump ridiculously fast out of bed as soon as I hear a peep.

That's what happened yesterday. I heard my name, sprang out of bed far too quickly, and hobbled to my son's room. After a quick change, downstairs we went to start brewing the brown liquid that would become my IV for the day. My daughter woke not long after, and the morning ritual began: making breakfast, packing lunches, getting everyone dressed, brushing teeth, and doing homework. My six-year-old was dropped off at school while my son stayed with me for the rest of the morning, as usual. He was a bit quiet, but we shared some couch cuddles, and that's when I decided to indulge in some much needed pampering. Yes! I would finally open that bathroom cupboard, filled with copious amounts of beauty products promising a better tomorrow.

I WOULD try that cucumber and green tea face mask!

I quickly sneaked into the bathroom but was soon interrupted by my little guy pulling at my shirt. Was he not feeling well? I picked him up, stroked his head, and peered deep into his blue eyes. Just as I was about to give the tip of his nose a kiss, WHAM, out of nowhere, he turned into something from the *Exorcist*. With my arms already in use, holding my once little boy turned 1970's movie demon, I was helpless with no means of blocking the sudden hot projectile spewing out of his open mouth. Remnants of lunch litter splattered my face, and there was nothing I could do but clench my lips tightly shut.

Moments later, my husband walked into the bathroom, stared blankly, and asked what the heck was dripping from my nose, chin, and eyelids. "Puke, honey. Good ol' fashioned puke."

After wiping off the hot mess, I realized the moment for my self-indulgent facial mask had passed. However, I couldn't help but note, after the veil of vomit had been removed, my skin had never felt better.

I had stumbled upon the best beauty product ever: a completely *all-natural* glycolic peel! And thanks to my son, last night on the news my skin glowed!

The Glow

For moms in need of some pampering.

You'll need:

2 oz. vodka
2 oz. chilled green tea
A small squirt of honey
5 slices of cucumber

Method:

1. Fill a metal shaker with ice and add the above ingredients, saving one cucumber for garnish.
2. Shake it until it's nice and chilled.
3. Strain into your martini glass, garnish with a cucumber, and plant yourself firmly on the couch (that cushiony island of salvation).

Toast to hectic days, comfy couches, and unexpected facials.

When Rote Goes Right

Sara Park

Have you heard of rote memory? I promise it's important to the story.

Rote memory is the ability to memorize information without necessarily understanding the context of that information.

People with autism, like my eight-year-old son Carter, excel in the area of rote memory. Sometimes people with this kind of memory will memorize random things like the credits at the end of a movie or a page from an encyclopedia. In my son's case, it's usually dialogue from a movie, an iPad game, or from somewhere on the internet.

He'll blurt these random lines out in a parrot-like manner, at the most inopportune times, when he's feeling stressed, overwhelmed, or anxious. His common phrases are *"Here we go,"* *"Nooooo,"* or *"Weeeee,"*—all of which he has picked up from watching YouTube videos of people riding roller coasters.

There is one video in particular that he tries to watch where one man screams "Ohhh sh*t!" as he's riding down the hill of a wooden coaster. I say "tries to watch" because my husband and I come running to shut it down as soon as we realize he has found that video again. The boy is an iPad genius, I'm telling you, but I shudder to think about the times in which that particular phrase could rear its ugly head!

So here it is, the breakdown of rote memory: blurts of random information or dialogue, inappropriately timed and out of context. At least, that was how it was until last week. Let me paint a picture of what happened.

Carter is our oldest child, followed by two typically developing sisters, Caris and Macie. The school-morning routine involves me driving our two school-aged children to two separate schools with a one-year-old baby tagging along for the ride. Macie, the baby, is not a great traveller, and on this particular morning she was exceptionally cranky.

I dropped Caris off at school first because she's the first one to start. Carter's class starts 40 minutes later, at a school a few blocks away from his sister's. We rolled through the nearest drive-thru, like we usually do, to kill time between drop-offs (hey, Mama needs her morning coffee!).

Three minutes later, with only 37 minutes left to squander away, we were back on the road again. I drove into the parking lot of Carter's school and put the truck into park. He likes to sit in the passenger seat while we wait for school to start, so up to the front he climbed.

Of course, with him up front, then his baby sister had to be too! So, I unbuckled her and she sat on my lap.

Carter and I made faces at each other, and we played word games while Macie played with the radio and the door buttons.

This is our usual school morning routine.

Except, *that* day, she wanted to play with the windshield wipers.

It wasn't raining.

You know when the windshield wipers are going faster than the rain is coming down, and they make that horrendous sound on your windshield? It's like: Nails. On. A. Chalkboard.

I told her no. And, well, she didn't listen. Probably because she's one. So, I sat her in the back seat again, and she started to scream a blood-curdling *I just stepped on a Lego mansion* kind of scream.

Carter covered his ears, because with autism often comes hypersensitive hearing, and she was *loud*. It was obvious that the volume of her voice was causing him pain, so I lifted her back into the front seat.

She was still screaming of course, but I was confident a cuddle from her mama was all she needed to calm down.

Nope.

She was losing her *mind*.

Rigid body, red face, flailing arms.

She was in the midst of a full-blown temper tantrum, on my lap.

I couldn't move her, so I tried to reason with her in my calm voice. Of course, she couldn't hear me over the sound of her own screaming.

I looked at my son, and he was looking back at me like *Dear Lord, make it stop*, so I reached for her blanket in the back seat, then her favourite book, her sippy cup, a flashlight—nothing was working.

NOTHING was going to stop this; we just had to ride it out.

I started getting sweaty, my hands were shaking, and I felt my anxiety rise as I questioned every parenting decision I had ever made.

My son said to me, "Is crying."

And I said, "Yeah, she is sad." (He has a hard time deciphering emotions, so I took the opportunity to explain her behaviour.)

"Macie feels frustrated," I said.

He looked out the passenger window. (I'm sure it was to plan his escape from our less-than-stellar morning.)

I reached into the back seat again to look for another form of distraction—anything to stop the madness.

Then I shifted my eyes toward my son.

He turned to look back at me with his big, blue, innocent eyes and uttered, "Maybe we should try a different route?"

Bewildered by the words that left his lips and wondering if I had even heard him right, I repeated it back to him in my own form of rote, "Maybe we should try a DIFFERENT ROUTE?"

And he said, "Yes."

Tears filled my eyes as I tried to contain my laughter. I have absolutely no idea where he picked up that particular gem of a phrase, but for the first time in forever, rote went right!

Of course, the baby was still screaming—she didn't find it nearly as funny—but all I could think about was how *hysterical* my son was!

He started laughing too, which made me wonder whether it had been a "rote" fluke or completely intentional, but either way, he was right!

My "ride it out" approach was not working.

We still had ten minutes to spare, so I figured I would drive around the block to try to calm her down. She screamed for eight of those ten minutes, but just as we had turned back into the school parking lot—silence.

The "different route" worked! It was that, or she cried herself into pure exhaustion and her tear ducts had dried out. Either way, she was silent.

Carter and I both heaved a sigh of relief.

Minutes earlier, I had sat feeling anxious,

overwhelmed and defeated, like I had failed entirely at this parenting gig.

My son has a ridiculous amount of rote expressions stored in his mind. It's like a Rolodex, but with random dialogue, quotes and phrases, all left disorganized, yet somehow it seemed he knew *just* what to say this time. His proper use of context and the hilarity of his timing lifted the weight of failure from my chest.

On that day, rote went so perfectly right.

The Cranky Baby

For moms who have been trapped in a car (or anywhere) with a cranky baby.

You'll need:

3 oz. vodka
½ oz. dry vermouth
½ oz. of cherry liqueur
A cherry, for garnish

Method:

1. Fill a metal shaker with ice and add the above ingredients.
2. Shake it like you're cranky and strain into your martini glass of choice.
3. Garnish with a cherry and enjoy.

Toast to YouTube, to rote, and to riding it out.

Inadequate Conception

Lori LeRoy

Being infertile is the best thing that ever happened to me.

Really. It might sound hard to fathom such an unusual statement, but it is as true as anything I've ever believed in in my life.

I was the champion of trying to get pregnant once upon a time—tracking my menstrual cycle in boring work meetings; drinking a sludge concoction of coffee, maple syrup and cocoa powder "guaranteed" to increase fertility; getting pregnancy-boosting acupuncture; having sex according to baby-making schedules from the Internet; and a host of other ideas that, in hindsight, were not the finest decisions I've ever made.

I once lied to my boss, telling him I had to run home to meet the plumber. It was really just code for hooking up with my husband for a quickie, after my fertility doctor called to tell me that my eggs were about to drop and to "get busy."

I was "out of town" a lot when invited to girlfriends' baby showers. I also developed an expensive habit of shopping therapy, buying purses and other things I didn't need, but which gave me a temporary high after checking the pregnancy test stick only to see one line.

In fact, "Operation: Get Pregnant" lasted six years and cost tens of thousands of dollars. The casualties were 1,611 prenatal vitamins, 78 fertility drug injections, 55 ovulation detection tests, 40 blood draws, 33 ultrasounds, 16 pregnancy tests, 11 embryos, and 1 gestational carrier. We were left with nothing to show for all the sex, money, weight gain, and heartache.

I grieved. I shook my fist, cursed, ate my weight in Twizzlers and Oreos, and drank Chardonnay with a straw. I even wrote a book about it.

After coming to terms with the fact that I wouldn't get pregnant, my husband and I decided that we were ready to move on. We really were okay. We tried everything that we were comfortable with, and we were at peace with all the trial and error.

Adoption had always been something that my husband and I considered, even before we knew we had fertility issues. It was never a back-up plan; it just became "the plan." So we put our hearts and souls into paperwork and prayers and sent our dossier off to Vietnam.

We had anxiously waited for 18 months when I received a call from our adoption agency that we had been matched with a seven-month-old little boy. It was before the days of smart phones, so I hung up with her and eagerly stared at my computer until her email popped up with pictures and more information about him.

From the second I laid eyes on the photograph of my baby, I knew I was meant to be his mother. It was love at first sight. To me, it was like the moment I had given birth and the nurse had placed him on my chest. He had a shock of black hair sticking straight up on his head and a brightness in his eyes that I'd never seen in another child. My son. The child I had dreamed of and had dreams for.

He was seven months old, and we were told that he would probably be home with us before he turned one.

My husband and I happily called our family to say, "It's a boy!" We prepped, we prepared ourselves, and I began to buy him toys and clothes with wild abandon, anticipating that we would be able to bring him home just a few months later. We named him Nate.

Then, we received some devastating news: Vietnamese adoptions to the United States were shut down just six weeks after we received our referral (when we received his paperwork and photos). However, we and 15 other families were supposed to be grandfathered in and allowed to adopt our children since we had already been matched. But regardless of the promise from both the U.S. and Vietnam to let us bring our children home, the adoption of our son ground to a halt.

Six months turned into a year, and the year turned into 15 months with no end in sight.

I would hear other parents complain about the dirty diapers, exhaustion from late-night feedings, and stains on their shirts, but I envied them and would've relished shit, spit up, and snot from my kid because it would have meant that he was home with me and my husband, where he belonged.

My mothering instincts kicked into high gear. That was my son, and we'd do whatever we needed to get him home. We hired a high-octane, amazing attorney. We wrote what seemed like hundreds of letters to government officials, celebrities, anyone who would listen and could potentially help. We got Senators involved (even the Secretary of State), and travelled to Washington D.C. We were interviewed by the media for TV segments and newspaper articles, and we organized Facebook advocacy groups and online petitions. It took three and a half years of fighting the U.S. and Vietnamese governments, but finally in November, 2011, we had a glimmer of hope.

We and seven other brave and resilient families left for one of the most remote parts of Vietnam on a wing and a prayer, and we vowed to stay there until we were able to bring Nate home with us. Five weeks later, we did. As much as I thought the best day of my life was seeing that photo of baby Nate, landing on U.S. soil with him in my arms trumped it.

I would happily go through the blood draws, hormone injections, mood swings, and weight gain again, because the way my family was created was better than I could have ever hoped for. My infertility led me to the children that were meant to be my sons (we adopted our Alex from China just 13 months after Nate came home).

It's hard to be a mom-in-waiting, no matter how a child comes into your life. Your journey may be filled with potholes, U-turns, and detours, but you can still have your happy ending. I love my sons as though they came from my uterus, and in that sense, perhaps, I am no longer infertile.

The Happy Ending

For moms who never give up.

You'll need:

2 oz. vodka
1 oz. passion fruit liqueur
A splash of sparkling water
A cherry, for garnish

Method:

1. Fill a metal shaker with ice, add the vodka and passion fruit liqueur.
2. Shake it like you mean it and strain into your martini glass of choice.
3. Add sparkling water, garnish with a cherry, and put your feet up until you hear: "MOM!"

Toast to never giving up on your dreams, to the fertility gods, and to happy endings.

A Turtle-y Awesome Valentine's Day

Abby Byrd

I usually shop alone, without my two-year-old, but every once in a while I get a wild hair up my ass and decide that taking him out for a shopping trip will be a special bonding experience.

Invariably, I'm wrong.

But his first Valentine's Day party—oh man! The excitement. And I'm talking about *me*. When I heard about his preschool's Valentine's Day plans, I couldn't wait to venture out for a box of those little rectangular valentines with punny sayings. You know, the ones where a banana says, "You're the best of the bunch" or "You a-peel to me"? The ones that kids have to put in every classmate's sadly-decorated paper bag, lest a first-grader be irreparably traumatized by having the fewest cards?

So one afternoon after school, the week before Valentine's Day, I picked Jack up and headed to Walmart. He had napped, and his caregivers told me he'd just pooped and been changed. I actually felt energetic for once. This was gonna be great! We sailed into the aisle of Valentine cards, and I started picking up boxes with themes I knew he'd like. *Thomas the Tank Engine*! With stickers! I'd print everyone's name very neatly and seal the envelopes with shiny red hearts. "Jack, how about Thomas?"

"Jack don' like Thomas," he stated matter-of-factly, even though this is a damned lie. He's watched it so much I can sing that dippy little tune in my sleep, and half the time I can hear Ringo Starr narrating my life. I should clarify here that my son constantly refers to himself in the third person, as if he were a mysterious oracle or lacks all understanding of pronouns.

"Yes you do," I said. "You love Thomas." I showed him the box, but he pushed it away. The same drama then ensued for *Mickey Mouse Clubhouse* ("Jack don' like Mickey Mouse") and *Teenage Mutant Ninja Turtles* ("Jack don' like Ninja Turtles"), even though he loves watching both of those shows. He seemed least offended by TMNT, so I was in the process of deciding between regular valentines and hologram valentines when a putrid fart smell permeated the air.

I looked around. We were the only two in the aisle. I made a mental note to check the school lunch menu and see what was on it for that day so I could make sure that—whatever it was—Jack never ate it again. Then he made a weird grunting noise, and I could just tell that he was shitting all over my idealized special bonding Valentine shopping trip.

I checked his diaper—sure enough. OK, Plan B. Idealized special bonding Valentine shopping trip would have to be cut short due to the potential of lethally gassing the other Walmart patrons. But I wasn't ready to make this monumental decision! The Thomas valentines said age 2+, but the Ninja Turtles ones said age 6+. I looked dubiously at the box, where the four turtles, in defensive battle poses, were brandishing katanas and nunchucks. What if this wasn't appropriate for preschool? What if the other mothers thought Jack a violent child and me an irresponsible mother? What if the other kids' valentines had little teddy bears on them?

The scent of fresh shit once again wafted by, and I knew I had to hurry. This was immobilizing—like when I wanted the last container of cookies at the Safeway bakery but hesitated because the label looked as if it had been tampered with, and I had to convince myself that a bakery terrorist hadn't opened the container and sprinkled ricin on the cookies. To kill someone. Just for fun. Ah, fuck it. I threw the Ninja Turtle valentines in the cart amid protests of "Jack don' LIKE Ninja Turtles." (LIES!)

We breezed through to pick up a few more items, and Jack was remarkably tractable, probably because he'd grabbed one of those clear plastic tubes filled with Reese's pieces and was gnawing on it. I let this pass because although I'm generally not in favor of Yellow 5 Lake and Red 40 Lake, I had a feeling both of us would need that sugar high to get home in decent spirits. Jack was not at all happy when I had to pry the tube of Reese's pieces out of his freakishly strong jaws to give to the cashier. I'm quite sure he sensed my frustration as I slammed it on the conveyor belt and roughly pushed the cart forward, because he then filled in for me what he obviously assumed I was about to say next: "DAMMIT. DAMMIT DAMMIT DAMMIT."

So, the kid in Walmart who smelled like shit and was saying, "dammit, dammit, dammit"? That was my kid.

And the kid whose preschool valentines have shurikens on them? Also my kid.

Nothing says "I love you" like a throwing star.

Chocolate Kiss

For moms who have their holiday plans shit upon.

You'll need:

1 ½ oz. vodka
1 ½ oz. clear crème de cacao
½ oz. almond liqueur
½ oz. cranberry juice
1 chocolate kiss

Method:

1. Fill a metal shaker with ice and add the ingredients (minus the kiss).
2. Shake it up and shake it off, like Taylor Swift (admit it, you love her).
3. Strain into your martini glass of choice.
4. Drop a chocolate kiss into the glass, pucker up, and give your martini some love.

Toast to embracing commercial holidays, ninja weapons, and public defecation.

When Do I Get to Slumber?

Kristen Hansen Brakeman

My husband and two youngest daughters were headed for the door when I noticed they were packed rather lightly. "Wait, where are your sleeping bags? Don't you need them to stay at your mom's?"

"Oh, didn't I tell you? She had a thing, so we're going to a hotel down in Long Beach instead. Thought I'd show the girls the Queen Mary."

"Won't that be lovely," I say, biting my tongue so hard it almost bleeds. It was my idea that my husband take our two younger daughters away for the night while our eldest had her first slumber party, partly to keep the younger girls out of their sister's hair, but mostly to prevent my husband from having that spontaneous migraine he gets whenever exposed to a gaggle of shrieking twelve-year-old girls.

Now I was jealous. Solo hosting of eight girls for 16 hours seemed like the better deal when compared to my husband and kids fighting for space on a fold out couch while my in-law's stinky, geriatric dog licked them throughout the night. But a night in a fancy hotel? That was a different story.

There was no time to dwell. Seven cars had already pulled up to my house. After a quick drop off, the girls' parents ran back to their cars, perhaps worried I would change my mind. The smell of burning rubber hung in the air.

"So, what are we going to do?" the kids demanded in unison.

Luckily, I had a plan. "We're starting with a game, then we'll have dinner…"

"Only one game?" a girl asked in a bratty voice. "I am *so* out of here."

I was horrified, but then she laughed, and we all laughed, and I remembered that my daughter actually had nice friends. I relaxed.

Six pizza boxes and two cartons of ice cream later, these nice friends were fuelled up and ready for action. The high-pitched chatter grew so loud it actually made the windows vibrate. The cat and dog ran for cover. I started to get my husband's migraine.

"Girls! It's time for a craft… outside! You'll be decorating these pillowcases with fabric paint. It's the type you can wash." Magically, the girls moved to the patio to start the quiet craft.

That was too easy.

The phone rang—husband was checking in from the Observation Deck of the Queen Mary where he and our girls were enjoying martinis, Shirley Temples, and the sunset. My youngest daughter yelled into the mouthpiece, "We're having a feast! Fried shrimp and nachos, and later we're going to have room service!" Great. Lucky you.

"Everything is completely under control here," I boasted. "What a great bunch of girls. Chloe has such nice friend—Kaitlin! What are you doing? Get down from the roof! Megan, did you… did you paint your feet? Good God, people!"

I threw the phone down and lunged for the future acrobat who had shimmied to the top of our patio awning. Then, I turned towards Megan and her purple feet.

"You can't walk on my carpet with painted feet… and there's paint on your pants, too! Didn't you remember that I said the paint was permanent?"

"Oh, I thought you said washable?" The kids, clothing strewn with various shades of neon paint, stared at me, crestfallen, as if I had deceived them.

"No, I meant you can paint it on the fabric and it won't wash out. That kind of washable." Apparently, I wasn't very clear on that point. I'll surely get some angry phone calls on this tomorrow.

One DVD, sixty minutes of Dance Dance Revolution, and three tubs of popcorn later, the kids were thankfully ready for the slumber part of the party. Ah, sleep at last.

Or so I thought.

Three hours later, and with cackles of laughter still emanating from the living room, I began to wonder if I would ever sleep that night. Surely, they would have to tire eventually. They were human, weren't they?

I pictured my husband sound asleep in that extra comfy hotel "heavenly bed" surrounded by cozy feather pillows and beautiful silence. My only consolation was that my youngest daughter would certainly wake him later in the night, convinced she'd seen a ghost.

By 3:00 AM, I had had enough! I marched into the living room, summoned my inner mean-ness and growled, "I don't want to hear a single word come from this room."

I'm pretty sure I heard someone say "word" after I turned the corner.

It was no use. I considered taking a couple Tylenol PM's. No, that would be wrong. The parents of these kids had put their trust in me. What if something happened in the night and I wasn't completely alert?

Hmm, maybe just one.

Two minutes later, morning came and my zombie-like guests were out the door.

I called my husband to tell him the coast was clear. "Okay, you can come back. The girls are gone."

"Oh, we would, but we're still waiting for a table. Apparently they have this fantastic brunch here."

As I was about to respond, I glanced over at my daughter, already asleep on the couch. Finally, I had a quiet house.

"That's nice dear. You take your time."

The Aftermath

For moms facing the sleepover aftermath.

You'll need:

2 oz. gin
2 oz. lemon liqueur
1 oz. fresh lemon juice
A few sprigs of fresh lavender
A slice of lemon
Sugar, for the rim

Method:

1. Place sugar on a plate, wet the rim of the glass with a lemon slice, and spin into the sugar.
2. Fill a metal shaker with ice and add all of the above ingredients, including a few sprigs of lavender.
3. Shake well, while trying not to fall over, and strain the energizing/relaxing mixture into your martini glass.
4. Garnish with some fresh lavender and put those tired feet up, while you promise yourself a real pedi, not done by tweens! Peace, *at last…*

Toast to excitable girls, sleep, and a quiet house!

New Parent's Survival Guide

Christina Antus

There should be a *New Parent's Survival Guide*, one that has all the tips, tricks, and secrets to doing it right the first time. Sadly, it's a trial-by-fire gig—one with no rules, just a lot of guidelines and spit-up.

A *lot* of that.

Parenting is full of moments that none of the *What to Expect* books cover. For example, there's no literature that focuses on the fact that your new baby will make creepy noises that you've only heard in George Romero films. Sure, there are books and articles aplenty that help guide you along, but after that, 80 percent of parenting is experience, 10 percent is common sense, and the last 10 percent is guesswork.

For example: Why does my baby sound like a zombie at 3:00 AM?

Experience tells you: nothing, because you have none. So your baby could very well be a zombie.

Common Sense tells you: since you haven't slept in six weeks, the only zombie in your house is you.

Guessing tells you: babies just make weird, creepy

sounds in their sleep.

So, here are a few of the most important things I learned on my own during my first few weeks as a new mom:

Disorientation and confusion are common. So is short-term memory loss. It includes:

- forgetting to move the clothes into the dryer
- forgetting how to work the dryer
- forgetting you *have* clothes
- forgetting to feed the cat
- forgetting you *have* a cat
- forgetting what day it is
- and forgetting what you were going to do in the room you just entered.

The memory-loss lasts for approximately the entire first year, although there's a nasty rumor going around that it doesn't ever go away.

You will have feelings of inadequacy. These feelings are not only normal, they'll get worse as your child gets older. Just when you think you have this whole parenting thing down, they change up the rules by getting roseola, teeth, or a taste of independence. Remember to always pretend to be adequate and experienced, because babies and children can smell fear.

You will sleep again. I know it doesn't feel like it. But one night you'll go to bed at 10:00 PM and wake up on your own at 3:00 AM. You'll race down the hall to your baby's room only to see her sleeping peacefully and grunting zombie grunts. Enjoy this time because babies eventually turn two. For whatever reason, two-year-olds don't sleep, because at 3:00 AM they need a drink. They want to know what the cat's doing. They have to find that one toy that may or may not even exist.

Babies are very slippery when they're wet. This caused me a lot of anxiety with my first baby. The ridiculous fear of handling a wet baby quickly transformed into a valid fear of dropping a wet baby. Use towels. Or gloves. Or tongs. Okay, maybe not tongs. Towels are great.

It's okay to hold your baby whenever you want to. You can't spoil a newborn, but a newborn can spoil you.

Baby girls can pee surprisingly high. They're also known to have frequent sneak pee attacks. After I had everything buttoned back up (which takes more time at 2:00 AM than it does at 10:00 AM), I'd discover everything was wet. Then I'd have to start over. It was like a cruel new-parent version of the movie *Groundhog Day*. Except, instead of groundhogs it was pee, and instead of Bill Murray it was me—with newborn pee in my hair.

You don't have to change your baby every time he spits up on his clothes. I did this. I had a lot of laundry. It nearly killed me.

It's absolutely okay to have no idea how many weeks old your baby is. Without a calendar, calculator, or counting on my fingers, I never knew how many weeks my first baby was. After eight weeks, I didn't even bother anymore. I just said "two months." It's easier for everyone, including the baby. Besides, it starts to get a little weird when someone tells you her son just turned 835 weeks old and will be taking his driving test next week.

It's okay to be afraid of the umbilical cord stump. Not because you fear accidentally bumping it will damage your child's intestines, but because it's gross.

Mother Nature didn't give you the ability to instinctively know what your baby needs. It's completely normal to not be able to distinguish your baby's cries until a few months have passed. The "I'm hungry" cry sounds a lot like the "my diaper's wet" cry.

Both of those sound frighteningly similar to the "quit giving me a bath" cry. Just remember the diaper goes on the lower end, and you'll be fine. If you put it on wrong, you'll get the "OMG! Don't you know what you're doing?" cry.

Bodily functions will become dinnertime conversation. You graduate the first few weeks when you go out and your partner asks you what's on your shirt. Without even blinking, you say "baby poop." The sad reality is you'll say it like it's the most normal thing in the world to have fecal matter on your clothing.

Everything smells like spit-up. Even if you clean your baby from head to toe. Even if your clothes are clean and her clothes are clean. Even if you move out of your house and into a brand new one. That smell is EVERYWHERE.

I cried a lot those first few weeks. I remember feeling like my world was turned upside down, and I had no idea how to make life normal again. I had no idea how to raise this baby or be a mother.

That was over four years ago.

I look back today and smile at that sad, frightened girl with baby poop on her flannel shirt and dried spit up on her jeans. I want to hug her, wipe her tears, and tell her that it'll be okay. I want to let her know that she really will get the hang of it, and soon it'll be second nature.

I want her to know two things. The first thing is: one day she'll wonder how she ever thought she would never get the hang of it. The second thing is: the amount of spit up she'll experience directly correlates to the intensity of zombie noises her baby makes.

The Exhausted Mom

For moms who learn the ropes as they go and know what should really be in those parenting manuals!

You'll need:

1 oz. vanilla vodka
1 oz. coffee liqueur
1 oz. Irish cream liqueur
1 oz. chilled espresso or strong coffee
A few coffee beans, for garnish

Method:

1. Fill a metal shaker with ice and all of the above ingredients.
2. Shake it like a *Mombie* (mom+zombie).
3. Strain this "energy-boosting" mixture into your martini glass and garnish, or not. You make the rules!

Toast to disorientation, exhaustion, and George Romero.

Tales of WTF?!

These crazy stories are written by some hilarious moms and are deeply rooted in ridiculousness. Each piece is followed by a delicious martini and celebratory toast for you and your mom friends to share. These unbelievable tales will make you laugh out loud, so be sure to sip your martinis with caution.

The Vagina Games

Lisa Webb

I think every mother can agree that you don't realize how much your own mother sacrificed for you until that magical moment where the paradigm shifts and you become a mother yourself.

Sure, there are the obvious things that you remember her selflessly doing while you were growing up—even if you didn't appreciate them. You knew she was giving you her time, her money, and the last piece of dessert in the fridge.

But that's not the half of it. That's not what changed her from pre-mom to post-mom. What I'm talking about is the sacrifice of her body.

If we think back to the days before motherhood, all of us moms can wistfully remember when our breasts were just a little higher, our pink parts and abdomens lacked scars from stitches, and we were free to jump wildly on trampolines without the fear of warm urine running down our inner thigh.

Ah, those were the days.

After my children were born, I was no different from

any other mom. I longed for some quiet time and for my jeans to fit the way they used to. But what I truly wished for was to be able to sneeze or do jumping jacks without dribbling in my panties.

Luck was on my side, however, because my kids were born in France. And you know how those French women are so perfect? They don't get fat, their kids eat everything, and they bring up well behaved children. Well, now you can add another item of perfection to the list: they have strong vaginas.

I know this for a fact.

Now, I may not have a French vagina by birth, but I have lived in France for some time now, and my private parts have received a dose of French nationalism twice over!

My daughters were both born in France, so hearing midwives and doctors shouting "POUSSE! POUSSE!" while my knees are up around my ears was nothing new to me. Having had my kids in France means that I received the same standard pre and postnatal care as French women.

After childbirth, the ladies of France take their pink parts (whether French-born or imported) for the standard six-week checkup. This is when I, like all French women, received a prescription for ten sessions with a midwife, or *sage femme*, to start my *"rééducation du périnée."*

Don't worry, I didn't know what that meant either.

So there I was, being all French. I had a prescription in one hand and a baguette in the other. I was ready for my appointment, my sleeping baby was in her carseat, and I had a big smile on my face, because I had no idea what was about to happen to me.

After exchanging pleasantries with the midwife, she handed over a little something that she said I could keep and to bring to each of our sessions. She called it a *sonde* (wand), but I liked to call it my joystick. You can take the words "wand" and "joystick" and use your imagination.

Wand in hand, we began our consultation. She asked me a series of very embarrassing and personal questions without batting an eye: *Do you pee when you sneeze? Can you have a shower without peeing? How is sex? Can you feel your husband inside you?* I wondered, did she really need to know all this, or was she just curious?

After our little Q&A session, up onto the examining table I hopped, and in went her fingers just to "check things out" up there. Now I understand that all women have had quick internal exams, but this was like nothing I'd experienced before. This was no one minute job! She stayed in there for ages, having me contract and relax for ten seconds at a time, all the while making polite chit chat.

The first time I was there, I must have looked terrified, eyes as big as saucers, trying to concentrate on this conversation (in French to boot) while we were possibly breaking world records for the longest internal exam. But like anything, if you do it enough times it eventually becomes normal. And, after a few visits, I would hop up on the table, assume the position, and get ready for a good chat with my new midwife BFF. We developed quite the "sisterhood" after many visits with her fingers in places where only tampons and my husband belong.

But that was only the beginning of the road down the path of the wonderful French vagina.

Remember the "joystick" she gave me? Well, after a lot of contracting and relaxing, her fingers were replaced by this magic wand. The wand had a cord on the end which was plugged into a computer. During our sessions, I'd get "plugged-in." The screen would come alive, and I'd be thrust (pardon the pun) into a gamer's paradise. That's right, I would start playing video games with my vagina.

It gave a whole new meaning to the phrase "plug and play."

On screen, I was represented by a yellow dot. The aim was to keep my yellow dot between the lines as it moved along the screen, controlling the movement by contracting on and releasing the wand inside of me, all the while receiving light electric shocks from the wand that were meant to strengthen my pelvic floor. Wild, right? I have to say, I got pretty good after the ten sessions with my midwife friend.

Fast forward two years, and I was back up on the examining table with baby #2 looking on from the sidelines. I was about to saddle up with my joystick for my final session of vagina video games, and I couldn't help but feel a bit like an Olympian in training for the Vagina Olympics.

The midwife was at the computer, turning up the level of electric shock coming through the wand, waiting for me to give her the OK. She started looking at me strangely as I told her I still felt nothing, she could put it higher. Hesitantly, she cranked the voltage a bit higher, and higher some more.

"I must have the world's strongest vagina!?!" I said with a smile. However my humour was lost in translation, and then she just thought I was weird. She told me that it was strange I couldn't feel anything, because it was on a very, very high setting and that she better not put it any higher.

Clearly I was ready to win the gold medal in the French Vagina Games, I thought. That's when I shifted slightly on the table to make a kissy face at my daughter, and—WWWAAAAAA!!!!!!!!

I released a sub-human sound that I was sure could be heard from the top of the Eiffel Tower. My body was electro-jolted into a starfish position on the examining table where I lay in shock. Apparently, my gold medal vagina just had the wand in on a bad angle. The midwife dove for the "off" switch and came to my rescue before I scared away her other clients in the waiting room.

It took five days before I stopped walking around like I'd just returned from my honeymoon.

Moms sacrifice a lot of shit, and their bodies are at the top of that list. Dads can't even come close on this one. Can you imagine a man tasering his "boys" of free will? I think it's fair to say that only women would willingly mildly electrocute the most sensitive part of themselves in an attempt to have just a little piece of their pre-childbirth body back.

It's been almost four years since I became a mother, and from day one, I haven't been able to sneeze without thinking of my own mom and sending her a silent "I'm sorry" as I reach for the Kleenex box.

I'll let you decide if I'm grabbing the tissue to wipe my nose.

La Tart Fleur

For moms with strong vaginas.

You'll need:

2 oz. vodka
1 oz. elderflower liqueur
1 oz. sparkling water
½ oz. peach juice

Method:

1. Fill a metal shaker with ice; add vodka, elderflower liqueur, and peach juice.
2. Shake your shaker and your derrière while repeating: "Ooh La La."
3. Strain into your martini glass of choice and add the sparkling water.
4. Feel grateful your vagina has never met "la sonde," and enjoy.

Toast to strong vaginas, the games that they play, and motherhood.

Bug House

Andrea Mulder-Slater

When my daughter was a toddler, she could whack a housefly like nobody's business. And when I say whack, I mean *annihilate*.

Wings. Guts. Everywhere.

When other parents were busy making sure their tiny tots knew their red circles from their blue squares, I was encouraging my kid to work on her gross motor skills with the help of a fly swatter named Smack.

Her natural-born tracking abilities were most welcome during the year we lived in a rental while our new home was being built. Our temporary place was an A-frame with large, south-facing windows and about 70 billion fly-sized holes in the walls.

We had a good system. My child would hunt, and I would help her ceremoniously flush her conquests down the toilet where they would (and I quote) "go to the fly fair" to be happily reunited with their friends and family.

And presumably their legs.

But then my daughter turned four, and just like that, the free ride was over. After witnessing the installation of a septic tank at our new house, my newly-compassionate child began to question the existence of the "fly fair" just beyond the crapper. With that we lost our live-in exterminator and gained a budding entomologist.

Not that there's anything wrong with that.

Except, everything was wrong.

I don't know how it is that I have a kid who is not the least bit squeamish about things that creep and crawl when the only way I can enter my bathroom in the summertime is with a full can of Raid in my hand, but it happened. I blame the Discovery Channel and the endless science shows I watched, pregnant and on bed rest, while I weathered relentless thrusts of hostile baby heels pressing firmly into my ribs.

I was always mindful of the fact that I could easily transfer my irrational fears onto my impressionable youngster. So instead, I feigned affection for creatures with antennae, thoraxes, and mandibles as well as those devoid of legs and oozing slime. I've read *I Like Bugs* more times than I'm willing to admit, and, while silently dying inside, I've enthusiastically worn the living worm "bracelets" and squirmy ladybug "rings" brought to me by my wide-eyed darling.

But when beetles and moths started to make their way inside the house (via the pots and pans from my daughter's play kitchen), something had to be done. When my mother and I spotted a Bug Playground at our local neighbourhood department store, we simultaneously grabbed at the box that promised hours of fun for five-year-olds like mine.

For those unfamiliar, a Bug Playground is a clear plastic wonderland featuring many sensational and exciting enrichment activities for beasties of all sorts. I'm fairly certain it's based loosely on the cages designed for cocaine-addicted lab rats. It came with an easy bug catcher devised to make wrangling backyard creepy-crawlies into the mini funhouse a breeze.

It was ideal. Except, it wasn't. This is how I imagine the Bug Playground came to be:

Bug Playground Designer: "The bug playground is complete! It's perfect. My best work yet."

Toy Company: "But there's no lock on the roof."

Bug Playground Designer: "Look here. It's got a pool. And a slide!"

Toy Company: "Really, shouldn't there be a clasp? Maybe a piece of Velcro or something?"

Bug Playground Designer: "Did you see the climbing wall? It's green. And I put a crawling tube in there. Look at it. What more do you want from me?"

Toy Company: "Yes, it's all lovely, but we see some problems arising with that roof…"

Bug Playground Designer: "It goes to market as is, or I put an end to the Spider Spa project right now. Trust me; I'm a Bug Playground designer."

Toy Company: "You're probably right. No one will notice we forgot the latch."

We didn't notice.

My daughter loved her new toy instantly and spent hour upon hour herding countless critters in and out of it while studying the accompanying guide. Some of the bugs made it back out, and others went to sleep. Forever. It was in this way that she accidentally discovered the Darwinian concept of survival of the fittest.

One night, I called her into my bedroom and asked her to bring along the bug catcher, as a nasty carpenter ant was making his way across my floor. She obliged and came running, Bug Playground in hand.

That's when it happened.

My sweet, lovely, innocent child tripped on her own feet. I watched in slow-motion horror as the box full of insects flew out of her hands, flipped upside down in mid-air, and came crashing down to the floor.

Lid. Wide. Open. Because: no latch.

Five enormous carpenter ants, one spitting grasshopper, two colossal June bugs, and a mini mountain of scuttling beasts—genus unknown—began to make a beeline for the safety they perceived to be under my bed.

Things began to unravel quickly, and I'm not proud of what took place next.

The jig was up as calm, cool, bug-loving mom morphed into deranged, get-me-a-match-we're-burning-this-house-down mom. I shrieked from atop the bed, repeating guttural chimpanzee-like noises, as my daughter stared at me in utter and complete amazement. Then she joined me, the two of us shouting expletives at the tiny beings making their way across the carpet.

She was bound to learn the F word sometime.

Mercifully, the six-legged inmates—who had been incarcerated for several hours prior—were moving like drunken sailors. Once I regained composure, capturing the ants and sundry with the bug catcher was a fairly easy (albeit entirely nauseating) exercise. Well, except for the grasshopper. Those little demons move like the wind when they're startled.

Since June bug legs stick to Berber like bubble gum sticks to hair, collecting those little fellas was a snap for the five-year-old who joyfully remarked, "That was fun, Mommy. Can we do it again?"

The Grasshopper

For moms who hate bugs but pretend not to.

You'll need:

1 oz. vanilla vodka
1 ½ oz. white crème de cacao
¾ oz. green crème de menthe
¾ oz. cream
Dark chocolate shavings and fresh mint leaves, for garnish

Method:

1. Fill a metal shaker with ice; add vodka, crème de cacao, crème de menthe and cream.
2. Shake it up, until icy and cold.
3. Strain into your martini glass—one that is not currently being used to trap a bug until Daddy gets home—and top with chocolate shavings and mint.
4. Think calming, critter-free thoughts, and enjoy.

Toast to things that hop, things that crawl, and things that are better left outside.

All Quiet on the Potty Front

Sarah del Rio

My son was four-and-a-half years old when my husband and I finally overran his considerable defenses and compelled him to renounce his allegiance to The Beloved Diaper.

It was a victorious day for us—one that put a jubilant end to two grueling years of what some call "potty training" but what I can only describe as something akin to trench warfare. The smells. The horrors. The nightmarish exercise in futility.

The *smells*.

My husband and I spent those years fighting desperately to advance across the no-man's-land that was my son's interest in potty training. There were times when we would go months without a victory, and it was all we could do just to keep the conflict from completely draining our mental and emotional resistances. Other times we would gain substantial ground, only to be driven back in a matter of mere minutes by defiant proclamations of "I hate the potty," "I want to wear diapers forever," and "I just pooped in the bathtub."

Because let's be clear—pooping was the cause of this Great War.

Our son had been a fairly quick study when it came to peeing in the potty. By the age of three, he'd conquered the regular-sized toilet, "just like Daddy." He'd become proficient at standing up to pee, "just like Daddy." He'd mastered the art of leaving brownish-yellow stains all over the floor, forgetting to put the toilet seat down, and absconding from the bathroom with a conspicuous lack of pants.

Just like Daddy.

Despite his comfort level with Number One, my son took *serious* issue with Number Two. In his opinion, pooping was *not* to be done in a potty. It was to be done in a diaper, preferably while squatting in a corner and hiding behind a potted plant. For two long years, our son stood firmly behind this belief, crushing any dissenting opinions with a mighty tantrum and a tiny iron fist.

Adding insult to injury was the fact that my son had *complete* control over his bowels during most, if not all, of this time. He was fully aware of when he needed to take a dump and he would alert me to it with plenty of time to spare. For all intents and purposes, our son was absolutely and 100% potty-trained—just without the potty part.

Son: "I have to poo."
Me: "Great! Let's go to the potty."
Son: "No."
Me: "Why not?"
Son: "I want a diaper."
Me: "I'd like you to try the potty first."
Son: "No. Diaper."
Me: "All I'm asking is for you to try."
Son: "No. Give me a diaper, or I'll hold it in."
Me: ". . ."
Son: ". . ."

Me: "I surrender. The battle is yours."

Because, you see, he *would* hold it in. He would hold it in *forever*. He would hold it in so long and so hard that no amount of water, stool softeners, or children's laxatives would relieve the constipation. Visits to the pediatrician were often necessary to resolve the problem. On one occasion, a doctor even ordered abdominal X-rays and then showed them to my son: "See all of this, backed up in here? This is poop. This can poison you."

These ominous words fascinated my son but accomplished little else.

I'm ashamed to say that during this two-year period, my husband and I came to regard our son as an enemy of sorts, an opposing force we had to confront daily on the battlefield. We saw him as a despotic demander of diapers. A totalitarian tyrant of turds. We cowered in the face of his daily bombardments.

We tried everything. We really did. From punishment to reward, from motivational speeches to expressions of disappointment, from compulsory potty visits every hour on the hour to just backing off and "giving it some more time." No matter how tried and true, our tactics always failed.

Sticker chart? Ha!

M&Ms? Get real.

Potty boot camp? *Please.*

We were slowly but surely losing the war.

Then, one day, after my son approached me and asked me for yet another Pull-Up so he could drop yet another deuce behind the parlor palm, something inside of me snapped. Maybe it was sheer exhaustion brought on from a frustrating, two-year-long conflict of wills; maybe it was just an overwhelming desire to be done with The War on Poop and all of its associated stenches, battles, and failures. All I know is that suddenly, in that moment, I went from "I'll do whatever it takes to get this kid to defecate in a bowl," to "FUCK THIS."

That evening, I told my husband that I was done with diapers. That I just didn't have it in me to devote myself 24/7 to potty training anymore. That our son could hold in his shit for the next twenty years and I wouldn't give a single care. I pronounced: "As God is my witness, I will never diaper our son's precious yet infuriating butt cheeks again."

My husband, who by this point had countless potty-training war stories of his own and a thousand-yard stare to match, agreed without hesitation. So that night, we put our heads together and developed one final, eleventh-hour campaign: Operation Diaper Fairy.

Operation Diaper Fairy involved gathering all of the diapers in the house, presenting them to our son, and informing him that the "Diaper Fairy" would be stopping by to collect them that very night. She would wait until everyone was asleep, put our son's diapers in a magic sack, and then fly all over the world, distributing the diapers to the little babies that *really* needed them.

And after that, there would be no more diapers.

My husband and I were less than hopeful about this last, desperate strategy. To be honest, we anticipated an absolute routing. We predicted tears. We predicted tantrums. We predicted pooping atrocities the likes of which had never been seen.

But none of that happened.

The day after the Diaper Fairy's visit, our son approached me and informed me of an imminent need to poop. He requested a diaper, which I denied. He requested I go to the store and *buy* him a diaper, which I also denied. He asked me what he was supposed to do then, at which point I directed him to the toilet.

And after a brief assessment of the situation, he actually *went*.

From that day forward, there was no more

constipation. No more accidents. All poops were evacuated into the potty with military precision. Concerns about our son graduating from high school in a Diego-patterned Pull-Up disappeared into a puff of grateful smoke, all thanks to the Diaper Fairy and a triumphant, conclusive, last-ditch maneuver.

The moral of the story, you ask? Simply this: should you ever find yourself cowering in the dark, dank parenting trenches, forced into a senseless stalemate with a tyrannical tot, the answer might very well be to just say "FUCK THIS" and go for broke with whatever resources you've got left.

Also, it never hurts to invent a ridiculous fairy and make *her* deal with the problem.

The Trench

For moms in the trenches.

You'll need:

2 oz. vodka
1 ½ oz. butterscotch liqueur
2 oz. apple cider
A dash or two of cinnamon
Mint, for garnish

Method:

1. Fill a metal shaker with ice and add all of the above ingredients, including cinnamon.
2. Shake it like you mean it and strain into your martini glass (because it's so much more elegant than a hip flask).
3. Garnish with some mint, exhale deeply, and remember that you're not alone in the trenches.

Toast to family, countrymen, and warm, dry socks—because trench foot is a *bitch*.

Sunday, Bloody Sunday

Dr. Jess Kapp

Have you ever had one of those moments when you were seriously concerned that your kids might be tiny little psychopaths in cute outfits? Mine happened one blue-skied Sunday at home in Tucson, Arizona. My boys were happily playing in the backyard while I busied myself in the kitchen. It was quiet, and every so often I would catch glimpses of their little blonde heads bobbing outside my kitchen window as they ran around in the grass—two beautiful boys against the majestic background of the Catalina Mountains.

I smiled to myself, thinking about what a perfect day it was. *See, my kids* can *do this. They* can *play on their own. They aren't always needy little noise-buckets draining my energy and sucking my soul. They are delightful little sweethearts enjoying the fresh air and gentle breeze of a warm spring day.*

About twenty minutes into my domestic euphoria, I noticed a sound that I couldn't place. It was not very loud, but it was distinctive. It was rhythmic. It repeated over and over again: a tap, or a small smack, coming from somewhere at the back side of the house.

I was confused. I was facing the back of the house and looking out my picture window at the mountains. I couldn't see any sign of my boys, but I could hear their giggly voices, and I had the impression they were playing sweetly together somewhere just out of sight. I let it go, figuring if the sound was the result of something serious, the kids would come in and tell me. After all, what the hell could it be? I didn't see anything suspicious, and I could hear that my boys were happy and somewhere within earshot. No reason to worry, right? I went back to my chores.

Five more minutes of this nagging noise, and I started thinking, "What the fuck is that?" It was driving me crazy. I stopped to listen, intent on figuring out why it sounded like something was hitting the back wall of my house at fairly regular intervals. That's when I realized that my kids' laughter seemed to happen right after I heard one of these smacks. I also noticed that their giggles—which had seemed so cute and jolly a few minutes before—had taken on a slightly more diabolical tone. In fact, they sounded maniacal, and it made me uneasy.

Off I went to investigate, feeling a little irked by the interruption.

I am not sure how best to describe what I found. My sweet, towheaded boys were stoning a small bird.

The bird must have flown into my kitchen window and fallen to the ground, stunned. It was able to stand on a rock below the window, just needing a few minutes to shake off the effects of smashing into the glass. But my boys had decided to use it for target practice.

The minute I saw what was happening, I lost my shit. The boys turned their smiling faces to me. In that split second before I screamed, they comprehended what a mistake they had made. Their little faces dropped as I let out a horrified screech and threw my hands up over my eyes. I hoped that when I pulled them away the whole scene would vanish like a bad dream. It didn't.

"What the hell are you doing?!" I don't normally curse at or near my kids, but this seemed like the right time to abandon that rule. I didn't give them a second to respond or a chance to explain. There was nothing they could say. The bird lay broken on the rocks, its tiny legs flopping in the breeze, blood coming out of at least one wound on its feathered carcass. I almost threw up. My boys did this. They were *laughing* as they did this.

My kids were serial killers in the making.

I couldn't get my voice down to a reasonable register. "Get in the house *right fucking now!*" came out as a barely intelligible, hysterical shriek. They dropped what pebbles remained in their sweaty little meat hooks and raced toward the back door, tears starting to leak out of their baby blues.

"Oh my God," kept coming out of me in my crazed, shrill voice. It caught the attention of my husband who came running outside to see what was going on. He looked at me like I was an insane lunatic. I pointed out the bird body as the nausea bubbled up in me again.

"They killed a bird. Look what they did. What the fuck did they do?" I fell to my knees in defeat. This was it: the beginning of their lives of juvenile delinquency and future crime sprees. I felt, in that moment, as if I had failed as a mother.

My husband calmly walked into the house. I jumped up and followed him, needing to be involved in the shit-storm that was going to come down on my boys. My shrieking started again, almost involuntarily, as I moved through the house toward their bedrooms. I couldn't stop screaming such things as: "How could you do that?" and "What the hell did you do?" and "Do you have any idea what you just did?"

These questions, too sophisticated for my five- and

seven-year-olds to understand, just kept coming out. I was desperately hoping a reasonable answer would come. It didn't. They just cried harder, and my husband tried to calm me down.

He was angry too, but he was calmer than I was. He went outside and gently scooped that poor little bird's lifeless body into a gardening trowel. But he didn't throw it away. He brought it into the house and took it to each boy's room, making them look at what they had done. "This was a living thing, and now it's not because of what you did," he told them. I was partly horrified that he had carried a dead bird into the house, and partly grateful that he was calmly (but sternly) showing them the consequences of their actions. What may have seemed like innocent fun to them had resulted in the death of a living creature, and they "got it."

His method worked. They cried hard and apologized to the bird. They told us they didn't mean to kill the bird; they had started tossing the pebbles at it to see if it would fly away. When it didn't, it became a kind of game to see who could hit it with a pebble. I don't believe they intended to murder that bird, but they did, and it broke my heart.

Since then, they have not murdered any more animals. I am now able to look at what happened as a one-time incident and not an indication that my kids are killers in the making. They are both animal lovers and gentle souls. But finding my kids throwing stones at a small bird was enough to strip me of all sense of reason.

Seriously… WTF?!

The Blood Orange

For moms on the edge.

You'll need:

2 oz. vodka
1 oz. pomegranate liqueur
1 oz. blood orange puree (equal parts honey, water, and orange juice)

Method:

1. Fill a metal shaker with ice and add all of the above ingredients.
2. Shake it like a mad woman and strain into a chilled martini glass.
3. Garnish with an orange slice (blood orange preferred) and enjoy.

Toast to sunny days, the joys of nature, and knowing when to question your (and your kids') sanity.

Bedtime Routine

Lisa Carmody Doiron

I have a slimy confession to make.

We can hear our neighbours through our baby monitor. We turned the monitor down the first few nights. We'd become friends with them, so it felt sort of sneaky listening in on their bedtime routine with their kids.

But a few nights later, Schadenfreude kicked in and we couldn't help but eavesdrop. Their toddler screamed "NOOO!!!!!" as the dad tried to feed him. Then we heard the mom's muffled voice as she took over. She made threats about never having sleepovers at Nanny's and no more *Backyardigans*. The toddler went from screaming to crying to silent.

Just when we were impressed with her discipline skills, we heard the familiar theme song in the background: "*Your backyard friends, the Backyardigans!*"

Huddled around the monitor, Husband and I were like dirty little school girls gossiping about boys. When the dad went to fetch his son for a bath, the boy shouted, "NO! I HATE YOU!" Our eyes grew wide with every toddler screech. We covered our mouths to stifle our giggles with every flimsy attempt to coax the preschooler into the bath.

I know what you're thinking: we're total assholes. But in our defense, the bedtime routine around our house had been a veritable shit-twister for months. It was kind of nice to know the neighbours were braving the same forecast.

On that particular night, our bedtime routine went something like this:

The baby's witching hour started promptly at five o'clock. I tried to assemble something resembling a meal while he screamed in my face. Stir fry. I went with stir fry. The toddler got hangry as his sugars dropped, and he howled.

Then I cried. Then we drank.

The baby had a bottle, the toddler had a sippy cup, and I had a glass of wine. We all calmed down and regrouped. It was quiet. Husband got home from work and remarked on what a peaceful day we were having. I fake-smiled at him and dumped the baby into his arms. The baby cried because I wasn't holding him for five seconds.

When we came together for dinner, Husband inhaled his food. I picked through the mish-mash on my toddler's plate pretending it was delicious so he might give it a chance. He was too smart for that. He had a tantrum because his meat was touching his veggies (it's fucking stir fry, kid, what do you expect?), and he couldn't work his fork. He demanded ketchup—not ON his food, BESIDE his food. I scraped the ketchup off his stir fry into a pile on his tray. He threw the stir fry on the floor and ate the ketchup.

The toddler's sugars spiked from the ketchup and he was HAPPY! He ran around banging into furniture and making animal noises while the baby continued to cry. I pretended I had to poop so I could hide in the bathroom for a while. Husband navigated the chaos as I snuck my wine up to the bathroom. When I returned, they were all quietly reading a book. I drank in the cuteness before downing my last gulp of wine.

We split up for bath time. I took the baby while Husband wrangled the toddler. The baby cooed at me like he hadn't just screamed in my face for the last hour and a half. I stripped him and made jokes about how he better not pee on me. He one-upped me by pooping in the tub.

After I cleaned up the poop, Husband bribed the toddler into the tub by promising him cheesies for his bedtime snack. The toddler complied, but he then did the dead-weight, limp-noodle move when Husband tried to pick him up. Once he was in the tub, he wouldn't get out and had another tantrum when Husband took him out. Husband had to up the ante; he promised cheesies AND juice.

The toddler ate his snack in peace while the baby chugged an eight ounce bottle. They both cried themselves to sleep while Husband and I plugged our ears and hid in the basement.

So you can see why we took comfort in our neighbours' misery.

After hearing their equally awful bedtime routine, we decided to engage in a new little bedtime "routine" of our own. We had efficient (yet animated) married sex. Six minutes later, we were fully dressed and glued to the monitor again. It was silent. *They must have gotten them to bed*, I thought.

Several nights passed and we heard nothing from the neighbours. *Maybe their son outgrew the baby monitor*, I mused.

A few days later, the toddler and I were outside playing in the snow. The neighbour and his son came out to join us as they often did. As they approached, I could feel the huge, dorky smile take over my face as I recalled their messy bedtime routine.

"HEY, NEIGHBOUR!" I called.

Despite my attempt to be normal, I could tell I had a glint in my eye that was sure to give me away.

"RIGHT BACK ATCHA, NEIGHBOUR!" he called back.

As he neared, I could see something shiny. One might call it a twinkle. Nay! It was a glint. He had the same glint in *his* eye that I had in *my* eye.

He couldn't trudge through the snow fast enough.

"That's quite the bedtime routine you folks have," he said.

My glint disappeared as I realized what had happened. *Oh my God. Not only did they hear our shit-twister of a bedtime routine, they heard us having efficient (yet animated) married sex. THEY HEARD US HAVING EFFICIENT (YET ANIMATED) MARRIED SEX!*

"You… were… listening to our… bedtime… routine?" I managed to choke out.

"Nah, not really," he said. "Only for about six minutes or so."

The Night Cap

For eavesdropping, sex lovin' moms.

You'll need:

2 oz. vodka
¾ oz. fig liqueur
1 ½ oz. white grape juice
A fresh fig, for garnish

Method:

1. Fill a metal shaker with ice and add the vodka, fig liqueur, and white grape juice.
2. Shake, shake, shake and strain into a sexy martini glass.
3. Garnish with a fig, turn off the monitor, and enjoy.

Toast to nosy neighbours, efficient (yet animated) married sex, and getting a taste of your own medicine.

The Scary, the Funny,
and the Ridiculous

Olga Mecking

We are in the living room of our apartment. Toys are scattered everywhere. They cover nearly every millimeter of the floor. There is hardly space to place my feet. My big girl is newly two and defies all laws of physics by flying around the house, climbing walls, and being in multiple places at the same time.

I am severely sleep-deprived, overwhelmed, and exhausted. I don't know who I am anymore. I don't know my name. I don't even know what I'm doing here. My big girl is giving me a hard time. She is screaming, yelling at me at the top of her small yet very strong and capable lungs. I've been spending too much time in the company of my children.

Wait, did I just think "child*ren*?" Plural?

Slowly through the fog of sleep deprivation, I remember that I do, in fact, have another child and set out to look for her. She's so quiet that in my exhaustion I sometimes forget she's even there.

I find her, though. I find her lying in the one spot in

the house that isn't covered by toys. She is still. Her eyes are closed and… there is a puddle of something red right under her head. My tired brain flashes with similar, terrifying images that I've seen in the media.

My heart stops. My brain goes into overdrive. My thoughts begin racing. *What did I do? I didn't pay attention, and now she's dead. My beautiful baby girl is dead and it's all my fault.*

I actually start screaming at this point. Please let this be a bad dream. Please let me wake up and everything will be fine.

But this isn't a dream.

The guilt is overwhelming. I can barely stand it. The part of my brain that really believes that my little girl is dead commences spinning and turning. It's busy thinking about how I'd notify everyone. It decides that I would say "there was an accident" in a voice heavy with grief. It actually starts planning a funeral. It wonders whether I would go to prison and lose the rights to care for my firstborn.

Luckily, that part of my brain is soon silenced by the more reasonable, logical part which had to struggle free from sleep deprivation, exhaustion, and shock.

It finally finds its voice, and its calming presence enables me to breathe again. It allows me to assess the situation from a more sober perspective. "Look," it tells me. "She's breathing. She's alive."

I see her little chest moving repeatedly up and down, up and down, up and down. I touch her little head. It feels warm, like the head of a baby who is very much alive. I reach down and stick my finger into the red liquid. I bring it to my lips and suck on it. It doesn't taste like blood.

It tastes like tomato.

I look closer and see that the texture isn't really blood-like either; it's more the texture of tomato juice.

And, if it looks like tomato juice, smells like tomato juice, and tastes like tomato juice… it *must* be tomato juice—not the best choice for children when it comes to beverages, I must add. The red liquid creates a huge mess and nearly gives me a heart attack at the same time!

But it doesn't matter now. My baby girl is alive! She is only peacefully sleeping. I will not have my eldest daughter taken away from me. I will not go to prison.

And now, I can breathe. The feelings rush in and I want to do several things at once. I want to call everyone with the news that my child is *not* dead. I want to laugh. I want to cry. I want to scream. I want to jump for joy.

Instead, I turn to Facebook, where I leave a quick status update so other people can laugh at my silliness. A friend comments: "Thank you for sharing. This is funny and scary all at the same time."

Funny and scary, she says. And she is right, because funny and scary is what motherhood is all about.

Being a mother is overwhelming. It's hard. It can be dark and lonely. But it is also filled with laughter, joy, and humour.

But mostly, it's just plain ridiculous.

Much time has passed since the tomato juice incident. We are all older, wiser, and more reasonable (or at least I hope so). We've been joined by yet another baby. The kids started school, and I'm doing much better now.

I don't buy tomato juice anymore, though.

The Bloody Ridiculous

For sleep-deprived moms with vivid imaginations.

You'll need:

1 ½ oz. vodka (omit for a mocktini)
3 oz. tomato juice
⅓ oz. olive brine (from the jar)
Tabasco sauce
Worcestershire sauce
Salt
Pepper

Method:

1. Fill a metal shaker with ice and add the above ingredients. You decide how saucy and seasoned you'd like your martini (or mocktini) to be.
2. Shake it up, while trying not to spill or create another bloody mess.
3. Strain into your martini glass of choice and enjoy.

Toast to the scary, the funny, and the ridiculous moments of motherhood.

A Baby, Broken Boobies, & Beastly Breastfeeding Battles

Kathryn Leehane

As the doctor reached over to my exposed breast and prepared to tear off my nipple, I decided I was done breastfeeding my infant daughter.

Actually, the attempted nipple ripping was the straw that broke the camel's udder. It had been a hellish five months of breastfeeding battles with my firstborn, and frankly, I'm surprised I made it that long.

I always knew I wanted to breastfeed, and I always assumed it would be easy (I'm not sure where I got that idea… MOM). Just stick the baby on the boob, and let the magic happen for a year or so, right? And, hello? Free milk! No need to buy the cow. Or the formula (whatever).

No one ever warned me of the potential horrors.

Although my daughter was born three-and-a-half weeks early, she seemed to know how to nurse. I guided her gummy little mouth to the right place, and she immediately went to work. As she sucked (and removed the top layer of boob skin) on that first day, my husband

and I delighted in the fact that she was getting her liquid gold.

On day two, a nurse came in to check my vitals while I was nursing. She gave my breasts the once-over, declared that I had flat nipples, and said that my daughter probably wasn't getting much of anything at all.

WHAT?! Flat nipples? What the hell did that mean? They didn't seem flat AT ALL when they were popping out uninvited in cold weather. Or in the shower… Or while swimming…

The nurse supplied me with a nipple shield, which I quickly discovered was not the weapon of choice for the superhero "Lactation Woman." Instead, it was a sort of medieval torture device for deformed breasts. As if having my tender ta-tas squished and pulled by an infant's mouth wasn't enough, I had to shove my raw, swollen areolas into little plastic cones with reservoir tips in order for my daughter to latch on correctly. It was like a miniature Madonna bra—except not at all sexy.

By the time I brought my daughter home from the hospital, my milk had finally come in. Unfortunately, she wasn't gaining enough weight. We brought in a lactation consultant who told me the areola armor was unnecessary.

"But the nurse told me I have flat nipples?" I questioned.

She shrugged, "I've seen flatter. That's not your problem."

That's when she explained that the pesky sucking reflex is developed sometime during the 37th week in utero—a milestone we did not achieve due to our daughter's premature arrival. She then introduced me to my second breastfeeding torture device: the supplemental nursing system (SNS). It consisted of a bottle of breast-milk that I hung around my neck, along with two tiny rubber tubes that I ran all the way down to my nipples and secured with medical tape along the way.

The contraption worked great when the lactation consultant was present. But when she left, I faced my next breastfeeding challenge. That SNS was really tricky to use by myself. Trying to get a newborn's mouth around my engorged, chafed, formerly-known-as-flat nipples, AND an errant little tube was incredibly difficult. That tiny tube seemed to multiply and transform into twenty spastic tentacles. It was damn near impossible to get everything in my baby's mouth at the same time. And her hands, with zero motor control, suddenly transformed into precision ninja limbs that would rip the tube, tape, and patches of tiny hairs from my chest.

One particularly stressful day, I was sitting topless in my family room, strapped into the supplemental torture device, trying to get my daughter's tiny mouth around the giant nipple octopus. My mother-in-law was sitting on the couch across the room from me. Her stare was alternating between my tearful face and my breasts. Back and forth she looked—amazed? Sympathetic? Horrified?

Finally she asked, "Have your nipples *always* looked like that?"

Not having seen my mother-in-law's breasts before, I could only imagine that she had Irish-pink, dime-sized areolas with miniature-chocolate-chip nipples (I really didn't want to imagine them for long). She was probably terrified of my dark, Italian-Mexican, bologna-sized areolas and nipples.

First flat nipples and now a circus freak-show? Speechless and not knowing how to respond, I focused my attention on my daughter (and saved the story for my husband).

The very next day, I got my first bout of mastitis—a horrendous breast infection. Basically, my chest was invaded by two searing-hot boulders armed with flaming knives that repeatedly stabbed my no-longer-even-remotely-fun bags. The doctor gave me some antibiotics and told me to nurse through it. So there I was, exhausted and feverish but dutifully taping tubes on my fiery, achy milk jugs and trying to coax my daughter to eat. And I was now self-conscious of my monstrous areolas.

Fortunately, after a couple of weeks of the supplemental nursing system, my daughter was finally successfully breastfeeding. Everything would have been fabulous except I kept getting mastitis. After the fifth infection, a new antibiotic to add to my allergy list, and flaky nipple blisters, I was determined to find the root cause. I dove into Internet research and diagnosed myself with a mad case of thrush in my mammary glands, possibly caused by antibiotics and/or milk over-production.

And that's how I found myself in the nipple-ripper's office, trying to get a new medication that would treat the thrush. Instead, that doctor wanted to rip off my nipple skin and put a bandage and some ointment on it.

Fortunately, I pulled my blistery nipples away from him in time, and I got myself to a different doctor who knew exactly how to help. He gave me the correct medicine and told me not to nurse while on it. So I had to pump and dump.

Apparently, the medication took effect immediately, because I had strings of coagulated milk coming out of my milk-duct orifices. And the clear breast-pump parts provided a front-row seat to the dairy disaster. It was like overcooked angel's hair pasta SQUIRTING OUT OF ALL MY NIPPLE HOLES.

Naturally, I made my husband witness the horror.

At this point, my daughter was doing just fine on formula. And, after a few days, my breasts felt the best they had since before I got pregnant. I cut my losses (and the guilt) and stopped breastfeeding.

A few weeks later, my mother-in-law, ever ~~obsessed with~~ concerned about my breasts, asked me, "How are your little boobies doing?"

Stunned but determined not to flinch this time, I replied, "You don't have to point out how small they are."

But she quickly retorted, "Well, they're smaller than mine, honey!"

Dammit. She got me again. Defeated, I walked away. When I later told my husband about the exchange, he said, "You should have told her that your husband likes your boobs just fine. Followed by a big wink. She'd have been mortified."

Fortunately, my husband does like them very much. As did my second newborn, who successfully nursed for an entire year.

The Breasticle

For moms whose boobs are survivors in their own right.

You'll need:

2 oz. vanilla vodka
1 oz. white chocolate liqueur
1 oz. butter ~~nipple~~ ripple schnapps
1 oz. cream
White chocolate shavings.

Method:

1. Fill a metal shaker with ice and all of the above ingredients.
2. Shake it up, like your mother-in-law isn't watching.
3. Strain into your martini glass and top with white chocolate shavings.
4. Give your breasts a nurturing caress and enjoy.

Toast to healthy babies, plentiful breast milk (or formula), and boobs of every size, shape, and color.

The Sweet Surprises of Childhood

Susanne Kerns

From a young age, my daughter was obsessed with stuffed animals. By the time she was two, her bed was so jam-packed full of stuffed dogs, unicorns, kitties, bears, and snakes that there was barely room for her. The situation got so out of control that we eventually had to add one of those giant wall nets just to contain the overflow so she'd have some room to sleep (avoiding the obvious solution of just not buying any more stuffed animals).

Interestingly, her bedtime animal entourage was not limited to just those of the stuffed variety. She had a couple of wooden horses which she carefully arranged so they didn't jab her in the head while she slept. She even had some plastic dinosaurs and alligators. Perhaps the most unusual addition was a gold-foil-covered, Godiva Easter bunny which she'd received as gift from a friend a few months before.

You would think that all of this company in bed would've caused too much temptation and not been very conducive to taking a good nap. But it was just the opposite. Her special companions were the perfect napping bribe *(If you take a good nap, mommy will bring Taco the dinosaur down from the net!)* and threat. *(If you don't take a nap, Zoe Dog is going to have to sleep out in the hallway!)*

And nap she did. Her naps were the stuff of legends in our mommy circle. She used to nap from 1:00-6:00, wake up for dinner, and go back to bed at 7:00. My friends used to refer to me as the *part-time-mommy*. Whenever I expressed concern to our pediatrician that she might be sleeping *too* much, he would threaten to take me out to the lobby and announce to all the moms in the waiting area that I was complaining that my daughter naps too well.

Touché.

I have to admit, the mega naps were pretty awesome. I had tons of time to get things done around the house and even sneak in some TV or a nap of my own. The only drawback was during potty training: post-lunch five-hour naps could be a little dangerous. But after the pediatrician's warning, I wasn't about to complain. After all, five solid hours of afternoon peace and quiet was certainly worth having to clean up an accident from time to time.

I had it pretty good until *the* nap happened—the one that will be etched in my memory for as long as I live.

My daughter had super-sized her mega nap that day, so I had to go wake her up for dinner. As I approached her bedroom door, I could hear some faint rustling from inside. *Oh good, she is already awake… but why hasn't she come downstairs?*

I gently opened her door. NOTHING could have prepared me for what I saw. There she was, sitting in the middle of her bed. Every inch of her, from her little chubby hands to the top of her head, was covered in gloppy, brown ick.

Oh my God! Oh. My. God! Yuck! So gross! What the? How

do I even begin to clean this? And the SMELL! What is that smell?

Is that… chocolate?

She stared across the room at me, eyes as big as saucers and a look on her face that showed she was even more confused and surprised than I was.

"MOMMY! My bunny is FULL of chocolate!" she said.

After months of loyal companionship, it appeared that the chocolate Easter bunny's secret identity had been revealed. And devoured. And smeared. Everywhere. Her little hands grasped what remained of the poor bunny's carcass—some torso and a couple of bunny feet hidden within scraps of chocolate-smeared gold foil. Her mind, I'm sure, was wrestling with the moral dilemma of how much she thoroughly enjoyed eating her friend.

She was too young to fully communicate the details of what had gone on during that nap/chocolate feast. To this day, I have so many questions: Had she always known he was chocolate and just feigned ignorance so her parents would be gullible enough to leave her alone in her room with a half a pound of chocolate for three months? If she didn't know, what was the progression of events that led to this discovery? Had the foil been slowing peeling away over the months to reveal the mysterious substance within? Or did the aroma finally get the best of her in one dramatic unveiling? And after discovering that one of her animals was "full of chocolate," did she then go around licking and biting the rest of her animals just in case?

I will *never* know the answer to these questions. My daughter is now nine and doesn't remember that fateful day when she ate her bunny pal. Despite the fact that she still has her bed (and net) full of stuffed animals, the only one that gets to keep chocolate in her bedroom around here is me.

Chocolate Naptime

For chocolate lovin' moms.

You'll need:

2 oz. vanilla, orange or classic vodka
2 oz. chocolate liqueur
1 oz. chilled espresso
Shredded white chocolate sprinkles, for garnish

Method:

1. Fill a metal shaker with ice and add the above ingredients.
2. Shake it like a kid with a chocolate buzz and strain into your martini glass.
3. Top it with shredded chocolate, wrap yourself up in a cozy blanket, and enjoy.

Toast to long naps, cuddly companions, and the sweet surprises right in front of our faces.

Just Another Day
in Motherhood Paradise

Holly Rust

Remember that song with the lyrics, "Momma told me there'd be days like this"? Or when your mom used to say, "Just wait until *you* have kids"? I do. Although, I wasn't really paying too much attention to these warnings, and I'm sure you weren't either.

Whenever we hear advice or words of wisdom like this, we often think: *people do this every day, so it can't be that bad.* Well, I'm here to tell you our moms were right! Motherhood is the hardest job on the planet.

There are days that are much worse than "bad" and should be termed more as "pure disaster." Luckily, along with the difficult days come some amazing moments. At times these magic moments are hard to see, and they typically only present themselves in hindsight, but thankfully they do happen. They help us survive motherhood—one day at a time.

I used to think I could have it all, do it all, and keep it all together. My tune quickly changed after my first son was born. Now, every morning, I just pray for a miracle.

Having to juggle several different hats at once is difficult even for the world's greatest magician, let alone a normal person like me.

As a working mom, the most challenging part of my day is getting my kid up and ready for daycare. You would think, as your child gets older and more independent, things would get easier. Not in my case. My child's growing independence apparently just gives him a license to argue with me about *everything*.

While running late (again) one morning, I rushed into my son's room to wake him. I was hoping this would be the one time when he would spare me the usual monumental breakdown and just follow my directions. I leaned in, slowly pulled his covers back and whispered, "Mommy is running late, so I need you to be a big boy and get dressed quickly today, okay?"

I'm not sure why I thought reasoning with him would work.

He reluctantly rolled over and asked me to give him a hug. What mom could pass that up, right? So I gave him a big squeeze and then motioned for him to go use the restroom. At this point, he was newly potty trained but still wore Pull-Ups to bed. I always sent him to the restroom by himself because whenever I was there, he would get distracted mid-stream. Wherever he looked, the stream would follow. The last thing I needed was to clean a piss pool up off the bathroom floor.

As he pretended to brush his teeth (by basically just swallowing toothpaste), I quickly applied some mascara to create the illusion I was well-rested. The bags under my eyes got a little concealer and my pale lips got a little gloss. As I finished my one-minute, better-than-nothing make-up job, I said to my son, "Now, please go pick out what you want to wear so Mommy can help you get dressed."

Now before I go any further, it's important to note

that my son went to a toddler school which required wearing uniforms. This meant he wore the same color of shirt and pants every day. Every morning, however, he had to choose between two of the same shirts and two of the same pairs of pants. If this didn't happen, there would be hell to pay.

"This one, or this one?" I asked, holding up identical shirts. As I waited on his decision, I could hear the clock in the bathroom ticking away. My anxiety was mounting. I was already fifteen minutes behind schedule and had to prepare for a huge meeting that morning.

After he chose a shirt, next came the pants. And just as I thought we were back on track, he informed me that his stomach hurt and he had to go potty.

I, trying to be on time, told him he was fine because he just went. Big mistake. He quickly started pulling his pants down and shuffling his way down the hall with clenched butt cheeks. Before he made it to the bathroom, he lost what looked almost like a baby animal out of his bowels. I then heard a tiny voice say, "I'm sorry, Momma."

At that point I didn't know if I should laugh or cry, so I think I did a little of both. I rushed over to clean the mess up off the carpet and noticed my Chihuahua had beaten me to it. So, I had a crying toddler, a famished dog fighting me for what he deemed to be "food," and me trying not to puke. During my efforts to clean up the mess, my dog stepped in poop and then jumped on me, and I then had to change into a new suit and burn the other one.

Looking back, I should've just burned the house down. That may have cleaned up the mess faster.

Keep in mind: my day had hardly even begun. Once I cleaned everything and everyone up, we ran downstairs for a quick breakfast that consisted of a granola bar. Next, I put on the four layers of clothing necessary to get through a winter day in Chicago. Then we headed out to the car.

My son—like most kids—hates his carseat, so the battle continued. I typically have to break through his planking across the seat with a karate chop to the midsection while endlessly begging him to sit down.

Once he was locked and loaded, I shut the door and let out a deep meditative sigh. I watched my breath mist in the cold air, thinking to myself: *This shit only happens in the movies, WTF?!*

I got in the car, turned the key, and then heard from the back seat: "Mommy I feel more poop coming."

Screw it. Daycare can deal with it.

We made it to daycare without further incident, and I arrived at work, utterly exhausted. I rushed into my office only to be met with a desk piled a mile high with files and contracts to review. I sat down and began mentally preparing for the morning meeting and the long day ahead. That's when a co-worker walked—leisurely— through the door with his suit perfectly pressed and a large steaming hot latte in hand. He greeted me with a chipper and friendly "good morning!"

I looked up, with eyes as cold as ice, at his well-rested face.

Good morning? Shut up asshole.

Motherhood Paradise

For moms whose mornings don't go as planned.

You'll need:

2 oz. coconut rum
1 oz. almond liqueur
1 oz. pineapple juice
A slice of pineapple, for garnish

Method:

1. Fill a metal shaker with ice and add the above ingredients.
2. Shake what your mama gave you and the cocktail shaker too.
3. Strain into a chilled martini glass, and garnish with a pineapple slice.
4. Imagine the peaceful sounds of ocean waves and gulls…

Toast to always being late, to cleaning up hazardous waste, and to just another day in motherhood paradise.

The Talk, the Face, and the Mile High Club

Kristine Laco

I remember the day my stepmother had "The Talk" with me. She was far too late, because I thought I already knew everything. I took the book and ran, red-faced, into my room and cried.

I never wanted to do that to our kids. I wanted them to hear the truth directly from their parents and for them to be able to ask questions, have a good talk, or scream out "NOOOO!" I wanted them to know that the subject was never off-limits.

My husband actually never had "The Talk" with his parents. He was forced to learn it all on the fly. I think he preferred it that way. I'm certain his parents did.

Talking about sex with our kids tends to be my department. Making stupid comments about sex to the kids, thinking they don't understand, is my husband's area of expertise. I have ~~cleaned up messes~~ had conversations with our cherubs about semen, prostitution, humping, porn, ménage à trois, and much more. Some were my husband's slip-of-the-tongue moments or double-entendres, and some were from bad movie choices we made as a family. The ensuing heart-to-heart conversations I have had the pleasure of initiating afterwards have all been completely comfortable* and easy to navigate for the pro (*completely comfortable might be a slight exaggeration—more like an out-of-body experience).

I giggled through "The Talk," on both occasions, mostly due to the face each of our progenies made. If you've had the sex talk with your own children, you know the face. It is a cross between "I am about to vomit," and "I think you are lying." It is a face that I repeatedly see when I am cleaning up the sex mess a movie or my husband has created.

For my husband, any mention of sex in front of our kids has been awkward, especially when he initiates it by accident. An example of my husband's mess-making happened one day last summer at the cottage. He, in his infinite wisdom, decided to point out two dragonflies who were mating in the air. "They're part of the Mile High Club," he said to our son, and he began to laugh.

The following conversation ensued:

Son: "What's the Mile High Club?"

Husband: *suddenly looks busy, averts his eyes away from our son, and is no longer laughing*

Son: "What is the Mile High Club?"

Husband: "Mile High Club? That isn't what I said." *still busying himself*

Son: "What did you say?"

Husband: "I said…"

crickets

Son: "Dad?"

Husband: "I said… the *MEL* High Club," (seriously, that was the best he could do).

Son: "MEL High Club? What's a MEL High Club?"

Husband: "It is a club that two dragonflies are part

of when they make the shape of an M while they fly."

Son: "I don't understand. Why is it called the MEL High Club and not the M High Club then?"

Husband: "Because… it reminds me of the Melbourne airport! I was trying to get some help one day when we were there… and all the staff had these name tags that said MEL on them. I didn't realize, though, that all the staff wore them. I thought the guy who was helping me was named Mel. I told this woman at the counter, who I thought was named Melanie, that Mel helped me until your mother pointed out that MEL stood for Melbourne airport and not Melanie or Mel. Your mom was crying tears of laughter when she said it." (This part was a true story.)

Son: *after a very long pause* "I still don't understand what the MEL High Club is, Dad. What is the MEL High Club again?"

Husband: *continues to be busy without further comment*

This is a clear classic fail. Adolescent boys do not get distracted easily when they are asking about sex, even if it is just implied sex. I was shaking my head and tearing up. My husband's explanation was so much more entertaining than actually telling our son what the Mile High Club was. Sure, it might have been a better strategy to go with the truth (or, better yet, to have never brought it up in the first place). But it was fun to watch.

Later, on the hammock, knowing that he'd been duped, my son asked the pro what the Mile High Club was. I told him. He made that face, then he laughed and asked what the MEL High Club was. "I don't know, son. I don't know," was all I could muster.

I'll leave that one for the man with the plan. The man who learned it all on the fly…

The Mile High

For moms who take care of the birds, the bees, and all the messy stuff in-between.

You'll need:

1 ½ oz. vodka
½ oz. peach schnapps
1 oz. cranberry juice
1 oz. grapefruit juice

Method:

1. Fill a metal shaker with ice and add the above ingredients.
2. Shake it like a sex-pro and strain into your martini glass.
3. Garnish with a wing and prayer and enjoy.

Toast to dragonflies, sex in the sky, and making it all up on the fly.

Wreck the Halls—A Tale of Christmas WTF?!

Jill Robbins

My husband and I became "empty nesters" (a term I hate because it makes us sound old and sad) in 2011 when our daughter moved out. To make a long story short, our solution to empty nest loneliness was to adopt two loud toddlers. My boys are four months apart and I'm so not kidding about the loud part. So, so, so not kidding.

Murphy's Law says that if you have more kids as a solution to that whole empty nest thing, your bird that left the nest will fly home again.

At least that's what happened to us.

So... traditional isn't a word most people would use to describe my blended, multiracial family. We're nothing like the Cleavers or the Brady Bunch, but when the holidays roll around, we're all about tradition. Clark W. Griswold ain't got nothin' on my husband's over-the-top holiday spirit.

Our Christmas season is about eggnog, sugar overload, and perpetuating the Santa lie. We go totally overboard with the decorations too. Remember that movie with Danny DeVito where the guy wants to light up the house so it can be seen from space? My husband wants to be *that guy*. We are elf-on-the-shelfing, reindeer dust-making, *Night Before Christmas*-reading, *It's a Wonderful Life*-watching, *Silent Night*-singing, old-school Christmas Purists.

Well, we are with the exception of Christmas, 2013. That one didn't exactly go so well.

We had apple pie-in-the-sky hopes for Christmas that year. This was our first holiday as a family of five, so the mantra was go big or... well, go big was pretty much the only option.

I like to call 2013 the Christmas of WTF?! because nothing went as planned, and the holiday left me slightly worried about how my boys would survive to adulthood with me as their mom.

There are a few sure things in this world:

1. Little kids get up at the ass-crack of dawn every day. This rule is null and void if, for some reason, I *want* them to get up at the ass-crack of dawn, but that's another story.

2. The kind of lazy morning where I lounge in my bed until nine is O-V-E-R. I might be in denial about this.

3. Two three-year-old boys do not "entertain each other." They squabble and make twice as much mess as one kid does (I know, you're thinking *duh*, right?).

Our 2013 holiday fun was eclipsed by the arrival of the Christmas Crud. We were all too sick to enjoy much of the festivities. I coughed and hacked my way through opening presents and spent the holidays with dirty hair and wearing sweatpants. For me, that's practically terminal. I'm a little high-maintenance when it comes to that sort of thing.

We munched on cookies and leftover chili and zoned out in front of the television instead of sitting down to a proper Christmas feast. I was much more excited about my stash of cold medicines than I was about my Christmas gifts. The kids were happy enough with their bevy of new ~~noisemakers~~ toys and instead of snapping a bazillion pictures of the holiday magic, I shivered under an afghan, hacking my way through a jumbo bag of throat drops.

I woke up on December 26th feeling like crap on a stick, so I allowed myself some extra snooze time. What little inner voice of reason I still possessed whispered this wasn't a good idea. I ignored that little voice.

My boys were in their playroom down the hall. The house was quiet. That alone should have clued me in to the fact that something was wrong. I mean, I'm not the sharpest crayon in the box, but I usually do okay when it comes to making reasonable(ish) parenting decisions.

But on this day I chose poorly. I blame the cold medicine.

My dear husband, also feeling like crap on a stick, decided to snooze along with me. My oldest was asleep in her own room. I burrowed my head under the quilts and squeezed my eyes shut in the hopes of a few more blissful moments of sleep. I convinced myself that my two sweet little boys were quietly watching a movie and peacefully sharing their stuff.

In other words, I was delusional.

Eventually, my hungry little darlings decided it was time for me to get up. I thought about pulling my usual trick of faking deep sleep, which would force my husband to get up with the kids, but I decided to be nice and let him sleep. Or maybe I decided I needed to pee, or that my kids actually should eat, or something…

I stumbled into the bathroom, foggy with the Nyquil hangover, and was greeted by the sight of a toilet bowl full of two, possibly three, rolls of toilet paper. The damn thing was gurgling. More TP was draped creatively over every square inch of our bathroom. I've never been in a frat house bathroom, but that is how I imagine it would look.

My husband always bitches at me for not closing the lid after I do my business because the bathroom is a land of inviting vessels of water for little boys. Closing the toilet lid might remove some of the temptation. But I never remember.

I decided I didn't have to pee that badly after all and climbed back into bed. I gave my husband a not-so-gentle shove and muttered a brief description of the bathroom situation.

"It's gurgling. You deal with it," I said as my head hit the pillow.

My man got up without much grumbling and went to save the day (or at least our toilet). When more yelling than I'd anticipated came from the other end of the hallway, I crawled from my cocoon to investigate. If the sight that greeted me in our kids' playroom were a Rockwell painting (as if), it would be titled, "Man Holding Plunger, Contemplating Child-Free Lifestyle."

My dear husband, plunger in hand, was standing in the middle of a Lego minefield giving two very contrite little boys the what-for. My little Picassos had colored almost everything in the room, including themselves. Themselves! The markings around their belly buttons and on their feet and legs resembled tribal tattoos. They'd removed their socks and pajamas to decorate and then gotten dressed, again.

Did I mention this was permanent marker? There'd been a mug of pens and markers on top of a file cabinet shoved in the corner. I'd had a few random *I should move that* thoughts, but I'd never gotten around to moving it.

Thankfully, Magic Erasers really are magical, and thankfully, we had some on hand. While my coughing, hacking husband scrubbed walls, I took my budding tattoo artists downstairs for breakfast. Their little heads were hanging in shame. Getting called out first thing in the morning for clogging the toilet and decking the halls with markers isn't a great start to the day when you're three.

Maybe I felt sorry for them. Maybe I felt guilty for sleeping in and leaving them to their own mischief. Whatever the reason, I decided to forego cold cereal. I'd make waffles and bacon instead! I sent the boys to the living room to play with their Christmas toys while I whipped up the most important meal of the day.

When I went to call them to the table, I found the box of tissues (that had been keeping me company) empty on the floor. My living room was littered with many, many shredded tissues.

I guess it was our day for paper products.

I sat down on the couch surveying the carnage of Kleenex. I wanted to yell but my throat hurt. My darling husband was upstairs with the Magic Eraser, and I knew that if he witnessed one more toddler mess that he'd probably completely lose his marbles.

I then pulled out my most brilliant parenting move of the day: "Kids, clean this crap up, or I'll call the Grinch and he'll take all your new toys back to the North Pole."

Yeah, there may be some faulty logic there. And, yeah, I'm sure there are some parenting books that talk about empty threats being a bad idea, blah blah blah. I tell you what, though, I've never seen a mess disappear quite so fast.

Obviously, sleeping in was a bad move. Sick or not, hubby and I should have flipped for it, or I should have realized that mom responsibility trumps Christmas Crud. It's a good thing we don't celebrate Boxing Day, because we spent the morning up to our elbows in plungers, Magic Erasers, and stray tissues.

Ah, motherhood.

No harm and no permanent damage done, but this series of kid WTFs makes me think there should be some kind of Parenting Common Sense Test out there. On the other hand, I doubt I would pass.

Christmas 2013 didn't quite fit into the box of what we'd expected, but that's okay. Growing our family means loosening some of our expectations about how we celebrate holidays and… well, pretty much everything. I'm learning that laughing beats yelling or crying, and sometimes you just have to say, "Screw it. Time for cocktails!"

The Perfect Christmas

For moms who… digress.

You'll need:

1 ½ oz. vodka
1 ½ oz. almond liqueur
1 ½ oz. eggnog
Nutmeg and a cinnamon stick, for garnish

Method:

1. Fill a metal shaker with ice and add the above ingredients.
2. Shake it, Ellen Griswold-style, while humming your favourite Christmas song.
3. Strain into your martini glass of choice, sprinkle nutmeg on top, and drop in a cinnamon stick.

Toast to breaking tradition, the wonder of Christmas, and the magic of Magic Erasers.

My Son: Evil Genius or Cat?

Kim McDonald

My darling son is pretty much perfect. He says please and thank you. He will eagerly give hugs and kisses and say "I love you." And, all is well… as long as nobody gets in the way of his plans for world domination. Okay, maybe he doesn't have the entire globe in his sights, but he certainly wants to be leader of *his* world. Or at least be the centre of it.

The kid is smart. Honestly. He pretty much potty trained himself by the time he was two. I cannot and will not take any credit for it, but it happened. One day he decided to just go potty and never turned back. Awesome, right? Yes. Except, this also meant that he had extraordinary control of his bladder, and he soon decided to direct his intelligence into dominating *his* world with the use of "chemical warfare."

This marked the beginning of an unfortunate phase in our lives.

Basically, my son became a cat. Not the cute cat that comes and curls up on your lap when watching a movie. No, I'm talking about the asshole cat that pees in your shoes when you don't open the appropriate can of Fancy Feast. This was, literally, my son. When he didn't get his way, or when he did not want to go to bed at—I don't know—bed*time*, he would pee on the floor, point, and tell me to clean it up. Get him dressed in clothing he didn't deem appropriate? Pee. Ask him to not climb on your head while trying to nap? You guessed it: pee.

All the damned time. Seriously.

This little habit of his was mostly saved for me. How lucky. However, on one particular occasion he decided to show EVERYONE his new skill. It was a bid to entertain the masses, to dominate, and to be seen.

He was successful.

My mom always hosts Christmas Eve. It's her thing—her jam, if you will. It means a house full of family and friends. It means lots of food, noise, wine, and people. Did I mention the house full of people yet?

Now that you've got a pretty good picture of the setting, imagine this: dinner was over; everyone was sitting around chatting and cooing at our baby girl and laughing at my son's "look at me" comedy. After all the wine, the crowd was pretty easy to please at this point. It was the perfect audience.

This was his moment. So, my little darling climbed up on to the coffee table and started to dance. A wiggle here, a coy smile with a twirl there. Cue the *oooohs* and *ahhs* from the crowd.

"Oh, how cute!" said Aunt Julia.

"He's adorable!" exclaimed Grandpa. "Look at him just climb right up there."

His baby sister was below, in her ExerSaucer, smiling and enjoying the show. I was at the other end of the room with Hubs, drinking wine, stuffing my face, and ignoring the danger. It was, after all, Grandma's house and the rules were different at Grandma's house, right? Besides, Grandma was standing right there, encouraging the show.

And then it happened: the WTF?! moment took place, then and there. His highness decided that not enough eyes were on him just yet, and he needed to have ALL eyes on him. So he pulled down his pants.

I knew exactly what was about to happen, but it felt like I was frozen in time. I just stood there, trying to use any Jedi mind tricks I had to stop it from happening.

Just don't do it, kid. Pull up your pants. Please. DO NOT PEE!

Turns out, I'm a terrible Jedi.

The next thing I knew, the room went silent as a steady stream of pee flowed from my son onto my mother's antique coffee table. A smile larger than Niagara formed on his face as he stood in a room full of people who sat wondering what the hell just happened. Some started to laugh hysterically. Others looked around in shock, wondering if they'd actually just witnessed a child peeing two feet from the dinner table and all over the lace table runner and the crystal candy bowl. Hubs and I looked at each other in horror.

Grandma immediately stepped in to take charge of the situation. She assured him and everyone in the room it was an accident and that somehow we all missed the sign that he'd needed to go. We should have been paying more attention.

Hubs and I looked at each other again. I took a gulp of my red wine and thought: *That, my friends, was no accident. That was the evil genius letting everyone in the room know who the boss* really *is.*

The Evil Genius

For moms in the midst of an unfortunate phase.

You'll need:

1 ½ oz. vodka
1 oz. banana liqueur
1 oz. clear crème de cacao
A banana candy, for garnish

Method:

1. Fill a metal shaker with ice and add the above ingredients.
2. Shake it like nobody's watching and strain into your martini glass of choice.
3. Garnish with a banana candy, remind yourself that someday you *will* laugh about all this, and enjoy.

Toast to family dinners, unfortunate phases, and laughing 'til you pee.

Acknowledgements

We are very excited to share with you Tipsy Squirrel Press' debut anthology *Martinis & Motherhood: Tales of Wonder, Woe & WTF?!* We have had such fun reading and working with these stories, and we hope you love them too!

First of all, we would like to thank our wonderful contributors (and not just because without them this book would be only two chapters long!). They have shared their mothering experiences with us through their expertly-crafted storytelling. Their words reflect rich and varied experiences of motherhood while also capturing those common threads—the ones that make us nod our heads with a knowing glint in our eye.

Thank you contributors for trusting us with your stories, cheering us on, and being true team players—whether you are a member of Team Wonder, Team Woe, or Team WTF?! We raise our martini glasses to you and toast to cherishing the wonder of our children, to triumphing over the days we thought we'd prefer to forget, and to laughing our way through the most ridiculous of disasters, which we will always remember. *clink*

Many people have given us advice, been sounding boards, and read parts of the book for us to make sure our martini recipe "research" wasn't interfering with our ability to form grammatically correct and structurally sound sentences. Thank you, in particular, to Barbara Day-Wills, Vicki Lesage, and Jocelyn Pihlaja for your editorial assistance!

We would also like to say thank you to our families for your unwavering support of this project. We'd also like to assure you that despite the closeness we share with our laptops, we will not have them join us for the next family photo shoot!

Thank you to our friends for your encouragement and enthusiasm for our book. We promise to come out of writer's hibernation to join you for some non-research-based martini-sipping soon! We'll even try to wear clothes that haven't been involved in a *WTF?!* mishap!

Finally, thank *you* for buying our book! We hope you've been able to steal some quiet moments to laugh, smile, and shed a tear as you read through the stories. We invite you to shake up your favourite martini (or mocktini) and raise your glass as we toast to motherhood and the tales we live to tell.

Cheers!
Shannon & Tara

About the Contributors

Tellers of Wonder

Alison Huff, "Best Laid Un-Plans"

Mother of Doom and Destruction, Alison Huff is a writer and artist who lives a country-bumpkin life with her husband, two kids, and two dogs in northeastern Ohio. She is not a morning person and arrives late to every event, much to the vexation of the rest of the world. A lover of lapsang souchong tea, unnaturally-colored hair, and Oxford commas, she writes her stories with a signature blend of humor and brutal honesty. You can read more of her essays on *BLUNTmoms.com*, and on her WordPress blog, *Please Stop Putting Crackers Down My Shirt*. Alison is on Facebook every day, and she tweets on the Twitter @crumbsdown whenever she has something to say that is fewer than 140 characters in length… which isn't very often, because she is terribly wordy.

Jocelyn Pihlaja, "Purse Person, Plural"

Jocelyn has been teaching writing and literature at the college level since 1991. She has a husband who cooks dinner every night, kids who hold up hands requesting "silence" when their reading is interrupted, and a blog, *O Mighty Crisis*. Her writing has appeared on *Mamalode*, *BLUNTmoms*, *The Indie Chicks*, *The Good Men Project*,

Mamapedia, *In the Powder Room*, *BonBon Break*, *The Mid*, the *Erma Bombeck Writer's Workshop*, and *elephant journal*. She also is a regular contributor to a local public radio program, *Women's Words*, where she delights in wearing huge headphones—and not just because they remind her she actually wore earrings that day. When she's not writing or teaching, Jocelyn can be found running on trails, exploring the green spaces around her city. Strangely, she calls this fun, even though she's usually lost, faintly concussed from a tree branch clunking her noggin, and wearing only one shoe after the other was sucked off her foot by an aggressive mud puddle.

Leigh-Mary Hoffmann, "A Mother's Wandering Mind of Wonder"

Leigh-Mary Hoffmann is a "my lifestyle" blogger from Long Island, NY, juggling a family, a job, and a busy, crazy life. She tells it like it is—the good, the bad and the ugly—and tries to keep a smile on her face and laughter in her life. She and her husband, Ernie, have a blended family with five children and a dog named Rosie. With that many kids, there is always something to laugh—or scream–about. Visit her blog, Happily Ever Laughter, or stop by on Facebook and share in the laughter.

Louise Gleeson, "Stealing Time"

Louise Gleeson is a freelance writer and mother of four living on the west side of Toronto—because saying it like that sounds much more sophisticated than "plain ol' suburbs"—though make no mistake: she fully embraces the perks of suburban life and has no intention of trading her minivan in anytime soon. When she isn't taking the kids to their various activities and compulsively filling their bento lunch boxes, she is a contributor to *Today's Parent* magazine, *YummyMummyClub*, *SavvyMoms* and various other parenting and lifestyle publications. She also writes an optimistic and heartfelt blog at *Late Night Plays* (so named for the only time of day she is able to write there) and is well-known for making her readers feel like they have something in their eye. She can also be found on Facebook, Twitter and Instagram.

Magnolia Ripkin, "The Donkey Is Strong in This One"

Magnolia Ripkin is sort of like your mouthy aunt who drinks too much and tells you how to run your life, except she's funny. Well, she's mostly funny. She writes an advice blog, *Magnolia Ripkin Advice Blog*, answering pressing questions about business, personal development, and parenting. Heck, even the bedroom isn't safe from her purview. She is the Editor in Chief and den mother at *BLUNTmoms*. Other places to find her: *Huffington Post* and *The Mighty*. Also check her out in the amazing compendium of hot bloggers published in *I Just Want to Be Alone (I Just Want to Pee Alone)*.

Angila Peters, "A Mother's Intuition"

Angila Peters is a Gemini who dislikes long walks throughout her home while stepping on Lego. She is also a freelance writer living in southern Ontario. She spends her days slapping peanut butter and jelly sandwiches together for her kids' lunches, and then she remembers peanuts are banned. She has been a writer since her pen first made real words in her coveted Scholastic journal. And by words, we mean she drew hearts with boys' names in the middle. Considering her expertise on young men, you'd think she became a romance novelist. But no, she went the route of a boundary-less blog called *Detached from Logic*. Here, she shares her struggles with mental health issues, parenting, and dealing with the obvious illogic.

Her big break came when a friend suggested she submit some writing to *BLUNTMoms*. So she did, and the rest is history. From *BLUNTMoms* came *Huffington Post* and being published in three anthologies: *Surviving Mental Illness Through Humor, Only Trollops Shave Above the Knee*, and of course this epic book. Angila believes in acting silly and not being afraid of what people think. This is why, at any given moment, you will find her children scolding her to settle down and stop being so embarrassing.

Lauren Stevens, "Life Is Like a Bowl of Ramen Noodles"

Lauren B. Stevens is a freelance writer whose work can be found on *The Huffington Post, Scary Mommy* and *Care.com*. When she's not chasing after her rambunctious toddler, Lauren writes hilarious and heartwarming stories about parenthood and women's issues on her blog, *lo-wren.com*. A contributing author for numerous anthologies, Lauren is in the beginning stages of drafting a memoir about her experiences as an Air Force brat growing up in Europe during the Cold War.

Shannon Drury, "Of Woman Grown"

Writer, at-home parent, and feminist activist Shannon Drury has been blogging as the Radical Housewife for so long that her first platform was Myspace. These days, she has traded up to her own sites, *The Radical Housewife* and *Shannondrury.com*. She writes a regular column for the *Minnesota Women's Press* that tackles feminist parenting, sisterhood (both literal and figurative), culture wars, and other fun stuff.

She has contributed to several anthologies, and her work has also appeared in *HipMama* and *Bitch* magazines. Her first book, *The Radical Housewife: Redefining Family Values for the 21st Century*, was published in 2014 by Medusa's Muse Press. Shannon is married to a swell feminist guy, and they share a house in Minneapolis, Minnesota with two kids, two cats, four computers, hundreds of vinyl records, thousands of books, millions of Lego pieces, and billions of dust bunnies.

Sarah Deveau, "The Saga of the Socks"

Sarah Deveau is the author of two financial guides: *Sink or Swim: Get Your Degree Without Drowning in Debt* and *Money Smart Mom: Financially Fit Parenting*. She's a prolific freelance writer, and her work has been published in *Today's Parent, up! Magazine, Parents Canada, Style at Home*, and most major Canadian daily newspapers including the *National Post*. She has contributed to dozens of parenting websites and blogs across Canada. After having the first of her three daughters, she opened and ran her own award-winning children's consignment boutique, Cater Tot Consignment, for four years. Today, she works in corporate communications and spends her spare time travel writing and trick hula hooping.

Tricia Mirchandani, "We Could Stay Here All Day"

Tricia Mirchandani is a freelance copywriter, essayist, and the blogger behind *Raising-Humans.com*, but most of the time she answers to 'Mommy' from her five-year-old daughter and two-year-old son. Her words have appeared on *The Huffington Post*, *The Washington Post*, *Scary Mommy*, *Brain, Child, SheKnows* and in *Pregnancy and Newborn* magazine. Tricia is currently writing her first book about how focusing on growth has changed her perspective on being a mom. She tells stories about motherhood, personal growth, and the life of a writer mama, because sharing words can make the world a better place. You can find more of her writing on *TriciaMirchandani.com*.

Cordelia Newlin de Rojas, "Abuelo in Our Hearts"

When she isn't writing, Cordelia Newlin de Rojas is busy raising multilingual citizens of the world. Former hobnobber with the intellectual elite, she is the voice behind *Multilingual Mama*. There she chronicles her parenting adventures while she, her husband, and their two daughters make their way across South East Asia. She currently resides in Kuala Lumpur, Malaysia, where she spends her time homeschooling her children and hacking her way through the urban jungle. Cordelia's eclectic and oftentimes regrettable past includes eco-innovation, sailing instruction, and restaurant cashiering. She contributes to *In Parent Culture*, BLUNTmoms, and *Mamalode* and is also featured in the upcoming anthology *Motherhood May Cause Drowsiness: funny stories by sleepy moms*. She has also been published on *Fast Company*.
Cordelia aims to finish writing her first book before her boobs reach her knees. Failing that, she hopes to appear

on the cover of *National Geographic*. For a taste of her Asian adventures, read her award winning post: *Twenty ways you know you are embracing your inner Thai.* Find her on Facebook and Twitter.

Lynn Morrison, "The Wonder Part of Wonderful"

Lynn Morrison is the mouthy woman behind the blog *The Nomad Mom Diary.* She's not afraid to admit that she wears sweatpants too often, fails at "sucking it in," and has, on occasion, hidden delivery pizza boxes from her skinny husband. From thought-provoking, to outrageously funny, to almost unbearably sad, Lynn's emotions come through loud and clear in everything she writes. You can follow her on Facebook and Twitter.

Tellers of Woe

Kate Parlin, "When Family Fun Fails"

Kate Parlin is a writer and mom of three girls, two of whom are twins. She is a former high school English teacher who now uses her love of words to chronicle her parenting adventures—the funny, the frustrating, and the infuriating—at her blog, *Shakespeare's Mom*. Her writing has been featured in numerous places online including *The Huffington Post, Scary Mommy, In the Powder Room, MomBabble,* and *Redbook*. Her essay, *Making Space*, was featured in the December 2014 issue of *Pregnancy and Newborn Magazine*; she was honored to be a cast member of the 2015 production of *Listen to Your Mother* in Bangor, Maine; and she is thrilled to have her work included in several parenting humor anthologies.

When she's not cleaning up pee or negotiating the putting on of shoes, she can usually be found hunched over her laptop with an enormous cup of coffee. Or a martini. It depends on the time of day. She lives in Maine with her husband, their gaggle of girls, and two ridiculous dogs. You can follow along with her shenanigans as Shakespeare's Mom on Facebook, Twitter, and Pinterest!

Shannon Day, "And, Brace Yourself…"

When she's not cuddling with her kids on the couch, complaining about the crunchiness of the kitchen floor, or perfecting her towel folding skills, Shannon Day can be found cocktail-shaking and story-making over at her site, *Martinis & Motherhood*. There she ponders the meaning of life while poking fun at her hot hubby. Shannon is a former teacher, a co-founder of Tipsy Squirrel Press, and a co-editor of *Martinis & Motherhood: Tales of Wonder, Woe & WTF?!*

She is a regular contributor to *BLUNTmoms* and her writing can be found in various online publications including *Mamapedia, Scary Mommy, The Huffington Post, Mamalode, In the Powder Room, Pregnant Chicken,* and *Sweatpants & Coffee*. You can also find some of her stories in print as she's a contributing author to *Only Trollops Shave Above the Knee* and *Motherhood May Cause Drowsiness*. Connect with Shannon Day on Facebook and Twitter.

Jen Dean, "'Seesh'—a Love(y) Story"

Jen Dean is a freelance copywriter and stay-at-home mom to three young boys. She writes a human-interest guest column for a local newspaper and is currently at work on a diet and fitness self-help book (strictly for her own personal use), a novel, and a memoir–not necessarily in that order. She has recently made the mind-blowing discovery that her Ch'i (Chinese for "life force") derives from all things "ch-" including her children, chocolate, champagne, cheesy poofs and Channing Tatum—again, not necessarily in that order. She believes *The Princess Bride* is the best story ever written, *The Wire* is the best television show ever produced, and that Dave Grohl is the bomb. She lives in the western suburbs of Chicago with her boys and her husband, John, who prefers to be addressed as, "Hey, Deaner," in an "Ali Landry from *Varsity Blues*" southern drawl (they were made for each other). You can catch up with her on *The Ch'i of Jen*.

Tara Wilson, "Double Trouble"

Tara Wilson is an always-distracted Canadian mom of three tween girls, living in the same suburban town outside Toronto in which she grew up. She writes about raising kids with autism and ADHD on her blog *Don't Lick the Deck*, with a perspective of humour and imperfect mothering. She regularly tries to host giveaways to rid herself of the raccoons that take up residence under her deck, but has been unsuccessful in changing the lottery and gaming laws. Also it seems that readers prefer iPads over dumpster-diving wildlife. Tara and her husband recently found out that they both also have ADHD—or maybe they already knew, but lost the paperwork—which finally explains all the times they took the wrong twin to the doctor. It also sheds light on why she was a terrible accountant, and was likely responsible for causing at least one client to go to prison. Tara is co-founder of Tipsy Squirrel Press and co-editor of *Martinis & Motherhood: Tales of Wonder, Woe & WTF?!*

She is a regular contributor to *BLUNTmoms*, *HuffPost Parents Canada*, and *momstown.ca*. You can also find her work at *The Mighty* and *YummyMummyClub.ca*. And you can always catch her procrastinating on Facebook, being too wordy on Twitter, and over-sharing on Instagram.

Vicki Lesage, "French Women Don't Get Fat"

Best-selling author Vicki Lesage proves daily that raising two French kids isn't as easy as the hype lets on. In her three minutes of spare time per week, she writes, sips bubbly, and prepares for the impending zombie apocalypse. She lives in Paris with her French husband, rambunctious son, and charming daughter, all of whom mercifully don't laugh when she says, "au revoir." She penned three books in between diaper changes and wine refills: *Confessions of a Paris Party Girl*, *Confessions of a Paris Potty Trainer*, and *Petite Confessions*. She also appears in three anthologies: *That's Paris*, *Legacy*, and *I Still Just Want To Pee Alone*. She writes about the ups and downs of life in the City of Light at *VickiLesage.com*.

Tamara Schroeder, "When the Shit Hits the ~~Fan~~ Wall"

Tamara Schroeder is a wife, mom, word nerd, runner, and lover of bad primetime television. She is still reeling over the fact the hospital let her leave with a baby for she would be responsible for roughly 18 years—twice. She compensates for the shock by drinking obscene amounts of coffee and wine. On her humour blog, *That Tam I Am*, she writes about her family life, pop culture, and her journey with anxiety and depression (it's a winning combination). She is also a freelance writer and editor whose work has appeared on *The Huffington Post* and *Family Fun Canada*. She and her family live in Calgary, Alberta.

Tamara is not suitable for children under 12 years of age. Don't tell her kids.

Brooke Takhar, "The Popsicle Doesn't Fall Far From the

Tree"

Brooke Takhar is a Vancouver-based storyteller and Mama of one goon. She runs so she can eat ice cream and blogs so she can make fun of her parenting mistakes. If you need a pen pal, gluten-free recipe, or a meaningless celebrity gossip partner, she's your gal. You can find all her exaggerations at *missteenussr.com*, her personal website for the past 65 years. Brooke's stories have also been featured on *BLUNTMoms, Scary Mommy, In the Powder Room, Project Underblog* and *Review 2 a Kill.* When she's not writing, sleeping or dumping black coffee into her corneas, she co-hosts a podcast with her brother: *I'm Right & You're Wrong.*

Spoiler alert–she's always right.

Carolyn Mackenzie, "Who Needs a Facial?"

Carolyn Mackenzie is an award-winning journalist. For several years she anchored the 11 p.m. news on Global in Toronto, Canada but very recently made the switch to morning television. You can now catch her on *The Morning Show* on Global.

She began her journalism career in 1999 as a Videographer in Nova Scotia and eventually made her way back to Ontario, where she joined the Global news team in 2005. Her husband is a firefighter in Toronto and together they have two children.

Carolyn REALLY embraces sleep but like most moms, gets far too little shut-eye. She loves coffee, smelling her kids' skin, a good loud laugh, that moment of quiet, Mom & Dad getaways, lazy Sundays, wood-burning fireplaces, clean sheets, and the words, "I love you." Connect with Carolyn on Facebook and Twitter.

Sara Park, "When Rote Goes Right"

Sara Park is a children's book author and illustrator. She is the mother of three kids. Her son is on the autism spectrum, and he's followed by two typically developing daughters. Originally from BC, Sara moved with her husband and infant son to Ontario in 2007. Her children's book *Clever Carter: A Story About Autism*, was written to educate typically developing children about their friends with autism spectrum disorder. Naturally, she is passionate about autism advocacy and inclusion… unless inclusion involves sharing her own personal colouring book with her children. She prefers a clean house, but prefers not to clean. She loves Halloween and burns way too much time and money on family costumes. She once enjoyed preparing meals for her family until preparing meals became making condiments from scratch. When her toddler naps, Sara blogs at *crcrsmommy's Blog* about life with her son and his overbearing yet compassionate little sisters. You can follow her on Facebook and on Twitter at @CRCRsMommy.

Lori LeRoy, "Inadequate Conception"

Lori Green LeRoy is a communications professional who lives in Indianapolis with her husband and two young (awesome) boys. She is the author of *The Inadequate Conception—From Barry White to Blastocytes: What your mom didn't tell you about getting pregnant* and the blog *The Inadequate Conception*. LeRoy loves traveling, running, horseback riding, spending time with family and talking about her kids. She is also an advocate of international adoption and orphan care reform.

Abby Byrd, "A Turtle-y Awesome Valentine's Day"

Abby Byrd mothers, frets, writes, teaches, and corrects other people's grammar in an undisclosed location on the East coast of the United States of America. Her work has appeared on *Scary Mommy*, *BLUNTmoms*, *Mamalode* and in *Scary Mommy's Guide to Surviving the Holidays*. She is working on a memoir about her decade-long search for a partner and why correct use of the semicolon may not be the most important quality in a mate.
Follow her on Twitter @AbbyBWriter, Facebook and at her blog, *Little Miss Perfect*.

Kristen Hansen Brakeman, "When Do I Get to Slumber?"

Kristen Hansen Brakeman writes comic essays about parenting and daughter-ing, or whatever happens to annoy her most at the moment. She's been published in the *Huffington Post*, *New York Times*, *Motherlode*, *The Washington Post*, *Working Mother Magazine*, *Scary Mommy*, and *LA Parent*, among others. She was also voted "Most Sportsmanlike" by her fifth-grade kickball team. Kristen lives in Los Angeles with her wonderful husband and three amazing daughters, and she works behind-the-scenes on live variety shows. She blogs at *Kristenbrakeman.com*. You can also follow her on Twitter and Facebook. Or don't. Really, do as you please.

Christina Antus, "New Parent's Survival Guide"

Christina Antus lives in Colorado with her husband, three kids, and two cats who still haven't caught the red dot. She's won a couple of writing awards, contributed to a few anthologies, and has been featured multiple times on *In the Powder Room, Mom Babble, The Mid, Pregnancy & Newborn Magazine, Scary Mommy, and What the Flicka?* She has also been featured on the *Erma Bombeck Writers' Workshop* and *MSN Living*. When she's not neglecting laundry or avoiding the grocery store, she's writing and making mediocre meals for her family. You can find her hiding in the closet, eating candy at her blog *christinaantus.net*, or on Facebook and Twitter.

Tellers of WTF?!

Lisa Webb, "The Vagina Games"

Lisa Webb is the author behind the blog *Canadian Expat Mom*. Five years ago, she and her husband swapped their home in Canada for an apartment in Paris. Now, living in the South of France with their two French-born daughters, her life has become beautiful chaos. When her family isn't in the land of wine and cheese, they can be found exploring the globe with far too much luggage. Lisa is currently working on her first book about her adventures in France. You can also find her telling stories about life on *The Huffington Post* and *BLUNTmoms*.

Andrea Mulder-Slater, "Bug House"

Andrea Mulder-Slater is a writer and artist living on Canada's East Coast with her artist husband, imaginative daughter, and folk artist mother. In a former life, Andrea was a public art gallery educator by day and a rock 'n roll journalist by night. These days, she splits her time between writing for humour blog, *No, Really*, running an art studio, sharing art lessons on *KinderArt.com*, and blogging about creativity for *YummyMummyClub.ca*. Her stories have also been featured on *Today's Parent* online. In her spare time, Andrea builds small suspension bridges and leaps tall buildings in a single bound. She sleeps far less than she should and has way too much useless information in her head. If only she could access it. You can follow Andrea on Facebook and Twitter.

Sarah del Rio, "All Quiet on the Potty Front"

Sarah del Rio is a comedy writer whose award-winning humor blog, *est. 1975*, brings snark, levity, and perspective to the ladies of Generation X.

Despite being a corporate refugee with absolutely no formal training in English, journalism, or writing of any kind, Sarah manages to earn her daily bread as a freelance writer and editor. She has also contributed to several anthologies including *I STILL Just Want to Pee Alone*, the latest installment in the national-bestselling *I Just Want to Pee Alone* series.

Sarah's blog, *est. 1975*, has won several awards, including Funniest Blog in The Indie Chicks 2014 Badass Blog Awards. She contributes regularly to *BLUNTMoms* and has made frequent appearances on *The Huffington Post Best Parenting Tweets of the Week List*. She has also been featured on *Scary Mommy, TODAY Parents, In the Powder Room, and the Erma Bombeck Writers' Workshop*. You can also follow Sarah on her blog, on Facebook, and Twitter.

Dr. Jess Kapp, "Sunday, Bloody Sunday"

Jess Kapp is a writer and geologist living in Tucson, Arizona, with her mountain man husband and two precocious sons. She is the associate department head of the department of geosciences at the University of Arizona, and she is also a senior lecturer teaching introductory geology to hundreds of less than impressed non-science majors. She writes a blog about everything from women in science, to motherhood, to the manifestation of her midlife crisis on her website *jesskapp.com*. She has written a soon-to-be published memoir, *The Making of a Mountain Woman*, about her transformation from sheltered suburban girl to bona fide adventurer while she was roughing it in the middle of nowhere, Tibet. Her writing passion is short stories that explore all the wonder, woe, and weirdness of midlife, one of which won the Society of Southwestern Authors writing contest in 2014. She also blogs for *The Huffington Post*. You can follow Jess Kapp on Facebook and Twitter.

Lisa Carmody Doiron, "Bedtime Routine"

Lisa Carmody Doiron lives in PEI, Canada, with her husband and two boys. She blogs regularly at *Momologues*—Soliloquies on poop, barf and postpartum depression. Her stories have been featured on *BLUNTmoms, Mom Babble, What the Flicka?, Mommikin and Mamalode*. She's also a regular contributor to *G! Magazine*. When Lisa's not blogging and mothering, she teaches music at a local public school. She is also part of a group of women lobbying government for better resources for women with postpartum depression in her province. You can find her on Facebook and Twitter.

Olga Mecking, "The Scary, the Funny, and the Ridiculous"

Olga Mecking is a writer and translator. Originally from Poland, Olga lives in the Netherlands with her German husband and three trilingual children. Her blog, *The*

European Mama, is all about living abroad, parenting, and travelling. Olga also enjoys sharing her recipes there. She is the editor of *Dutched Up,* an anthology of essays about living in the Netherlands as an expat woman. She regularly contributes to *BLUNTmoms, World Moms Blog,* and *Multicultural Kid Blogs.* Her writing has been published on *Scary Mommy, The Huffington Post* and *Mamalode.* When not blogging, or thinking about blogging, Olga can be found reading, drinking tea… and reading some more.

Kathryn Leehane, "A Baby, Broken Boobies, & Beastly Breastfeeding Battles"

Kathryn Leehane is a writer, humorist, and storyteller. She's penned essays ranging from ridiculously silly to heartbreakingly serious that have been featured on sites such as *BLUNTmoms, Erma Bombeck Writers' Workshop, The Huffington Post,* and *Scary Mommy.* She is also the voice behind the humor blog *Foxy Wine Pocket,* where she shares twisted (and only sometimes exaggerated and inappropriate) stories about life as a mother, wife, friend, and wine-drinker. She is a contributing author to several anthologies and is at work on her first manuscript—a memoir about loss and survival. In her down time, she inhales books, bacon, and Oregon Pinot Noir, and her interests include over-sharing, Jason Bateman, and crashing high school reunions. Connect with her on Facebook and Twitter.

Susanne Kerns, "The Sweet Surprises of Childhood"

Once upon a time, Susanne Kerns was a Senior Account Director at an advertising agency working for two of the top brands in the world. Nine years ago, she traded in her corporate life for a life as a stay-at-home mom, raising two of the best kids in the world. She started her blog, *The Dusty Parachute*, as a way to dust off her online advertising skills and begin her job search. Instead, she now uses it as a way to spend lots of time on the computer so her kids think that Mommy has a job. Susanne's essays have been featured on *Scary Mommy*, *BonBon Break*, and *Redbook* and she is also a contributor in the upcoming book, *It's Really 10 Months, Special Delivery*. You can follow her on Facebook, Instagram and Twitter.

Holly Rust, "Just Another Day in Motherhood Paradise"

Holly Rust is a native Texan, but she is currently living (and freezing) in the great city of Chicago with her husband, two sons, and a Chihuahua. Aside from chasing around two lunatic toddlers all day, she is a professional writer and business consultant. She is the co-founder of a popular humor blog, *Mother's Guide To Sanity*, which has been featured on *The TODAY Show* blog. She is also a regular contributing writer for *The Huffington Post, Scary Mommy, Dot Complicated* and *The TODAY Parenting Team*. You can find her essays published in several anthologies, too! Follow her random thoughts on Facebook and Twitter–but no judging.

Kristine Laco, "The Talk, the Face, and the Mile High Club"

Kristine Laco writes a blog called *Mum Revised* and has been successfully keeping two children and a dog alive in Toronto for quite some time. Kristine shares the stories we all have with a splash of sarcasm, a pinch of bitch, and a ton of wine. She takes selfies at the gynecologist's office, makes Taco Tuesday her gospel, and knows that reality TV is real, folks. Her middle finger is her favourite, and she lives by the motto that if you are not yelling at your kids, you are not spending enough time with them. You can also find Kristine at *BLUNTmoms*, in an upcoming anthology *How To Survive Tantrums and Babysitters*, or on the couch hogging the remote. You can find Kristine on Facebook and Twitter.

Jill Robbins, "Wreck the Halls—A Tale of Christmas WTF?!"

Jill Robbins is a wannabe wine snob and sometimes runner from San Antonio, Texas. She has a degree in social psychology which has so far been unhelpful in understanding the behavior of her husband and three children. She writes about adoption, motherhood, and midlife on her blog, *Ripped Jeans and Bifocals*. Jill is a regular contributor to *The Huffington Post, BLUNTmoms, Babble*, and *Mamalode*. She's also been published in *The Washington Post's On Parenting* and is a proud member of the 2015 cast of *Listen to Your Mother, Austin*. Her work has also been featured on *Scary Mommy, Mamapedia Voices, In the Powder Room, SheKnows Parenting, Midlife Boulevard, Beyond Your Blog* and other places around the internet. Her print publications include the December 2014 issue of *Mamalode* and three upcoming anthologies about motherhood. She someday hopes to write the books that are living in her head. You can follow Jill on Facebook and Twitter.

Kim McDonald, "My Son: Evil Genius or Cat?"

Kim McDonald is on a mission to share the good, the bad, and the ugly side of parenting. She is a wine-loving, sarcasm-throwing Canadian mom who writes at *Two Bugs and a Blog*, works at a job she loves but with hours she hates, and sometimes even spends time with her kids (even if it means having a dinner of crackers and cheese with ham on the side). Kim has been known to release her inner beast when discussion topics (that she never knew mattered until becoming a parent) are shoved in her face. You can often find her at the playground, parenting from afar while keeping up to date on all the latest celebrity family gossip; still keeping track of her loving, handsome, but somewhat dim-witted husband; and still catching her daredevils while they superman off the slide.

You can also find her cheering on her Flames while keeping her Habs-crazed husband from brainwashing their kids. She has written for *BLUNTmoms, Parentdish, and Urban Infant*. Her greatest goal when becoming an incredibly part-time blogger was to one day be published. Mission accomplished! Next, she's off to figure out how to get her kids to actually take her seriously when she tells them that the sleep monster will come and eat them if they don't go to sleep and let Mommy watch Netflix in peace. Some things are harder than others. Follow Kim on Facebook.

21030482R00143

Made in the USA
Middletown, DE
17 June 2015